LANDSCAPE DESIGN FOR ARCHITECTURAL STYLE

VOLUME ONE:
EUROPEAN INFLUENCED

SCOTT BRADSTREET

Schiffer Publishing Ltd®
4880 Lower Valley Road Atglen Pennsylvania 19310
Printed in China

Disclaimer and Acknowledgment of Trademarks

Most of the items and products in this book may be covered by various copyrights, trademarks, and logotypes. Their use herein is for identification purposes only. All rights are reserved by their respective owners.

The text and products pictured in this book are from the collection of the author of this book, its publisher, or various private parties. This book is not sponsored, endorsed or otherwise affiliated with any of the companies whose products are represented herein. This book is derived from the author's independent research.

Other Schiffer Books on Related Subjects

1000 Fences and Gates. Jo Cryder. ISBN: 0-7643-2409-8. $24.95.
Designs for Garden Paths. Heidi Howcroft. ISBN: 0-7643-0383-X. $29.95.
Fences, Gates & Walls. Ashley Rooney. ISBN: 978-0-7643-2643-1. $24.95.
Garden Ornaments and Antiques. Myra Yellin Outwater & Eric B. Outwater. ISBN: 0-7643-1125-5. $39.95.
Paver Projects: Designs for Amazing Outdoor Environments. Melissa Cardona, PaverModule. ISBN: 0-7643-2345-8. $29.95.
Retaining Walls: A Building Guide and Design Gallery. National Concrete Masonry Association Tina Skinner. ISBN: 0-7643-1836-5. $24.95.
Sky Gardens. Signe Nielsen. ISBN: 0764320041. $39.95.
Victorian Gardens. Caroline Holmes. ISBN: 0-7643-1889-6. $29.95.

Library of Congress Control Number: 2008933699

Designed by John P. Cheek
Cover design by Bruce Waters
Type set in Trajan Pro/Zurich BT

ISBN: 978-0-7643-3106-0
Printed in China

Schiffer Books are available at special discounts for bulk purchases for sales promotions or premiums. Special editions, including personalized covers, corporate imprints, and excerpts can be created in large quantities for special needs. For more information contact the publisher:

Published by Schiffer Publishing Ltd.
4880 Lower Valley Road
Atglen, PA 19310
Phone: (610) 593-1777; Fax: (610) 593-2002
E-mail: Info@schifferbooks.com

For the largest selection of fine reference books on this and related subjects, please visit our web site at
www.schifferbooks.com
We are always looking for people to write books on new and related subjects. If you have an idea for a book please contact us at the above address.

This book may be purchased from the publisher.
Include $5.00 for shipping.
Please try your bookstore first.
You may write for a free catalog.

In Europe, Schiffer books are distributed by
Bushwood Books
6 Marksbury Ave.
Kew Gardens
Surrey TW9 4JF England
Phone: 44 (0) 20 8392-8585; Fax: 44 (0) 20 8392-9876
E-mail: info@bushwoodbooks.co.uk
Website: www.bushwoodbooks.co.uk
Free postage in the U.K., Europe; air mail at cost.

Dedication

This book is dedicated to my parents, Vern and Vickie Bradstreet. My father was named after his grandfather, a lumberjack who lost his life when he was struck by a tree. How ironic, a man killed by a tree is survived by a descendant who is a landscape architect!

Acknowledgments

Thank you Schiffer Publishing and Tina Skinner for being willing to take a chance on me and my first endeavor as a writer.

This book is the product of seven years of dreaming, reading, sketching, photographing, and writing, with many valleys and peaks in both energy and hope. In the past seven years, many family vacations have been planned to places where photos could be captured. Many weekends and nights have been spent with sketchpads or a laptop in the family room. Thank God for my family, Karen, Derek, and Austin Bradstreet, who have put up with me during the crazy bursts of inspired writing and during the tough days of the journey when it seemed this thing would never be done.

Other people who have made this possible, whether for content or moral support, are Carol MacDonald, Loren Pluth, Nancy Palmer, Todd and Judy Bradstreet, Vern and Vickie Bradstreet, Tammi Strasen, Jeff Hutchins, Adam Anderson, Daniel Miller, Megan Flanagan, John Cahill, Mark Steyaert, David Ling, Scott Ulrich, Peter Beers, and Bob Weston.

Also to thank are the Hoftmans; the Friebes; the Fulimers; the Domines'; Wimmer, Yamada, and Caughey; Land ArcWest; Lynn Lapouya Inc.; Conceptual Design and Planning Company; and Ridge Landscape Architects.

Organizations that have made photographic contributions are the Queen Victoria Inn Bed & Breakfast and Doug McCain, Innkeeper; the Carson Mansion, Eureka Heritage Society, and Ron Kuhnel; the Abbey Bed and Breakfast and Jay Schatz; The Hotel Windsor and Zachary Broomhall; Whaley House Museum; Frank Lloyd Wright Preservation Trust; Winchester Mystery House; Country French Bed and Breakfast; the Gingerbread Inn, Joan and Fred Echevarria; the Shaw House; Victorian Lace Inn and Andrew O'Sullivan; La Belle Epoque; Halycon Inn and Mary Floyd, Innkeeper, Owner; Carter House Inns and Audrey Archibald, Manager; and Inn at 22 Jackson Street and Suzanne Meyers.

CONTENTS

FOREWORD

If you have been in or around the profession of landscape architecture for very long, you have probably noticed the void I noticed. Many books have been written about the various architectural styles for buildings and there are many books relating individual architectural styles to "garden design," but no book or series of books exists providing a complete guide for creating site elements and landscape design for most major architectural styles.

In the past, developers and owners have always had the choice to design buildings based upon a particular architectural style and have had the choice to include a corresponding landscape design. Recently, architectural design has increasingly become more important to governing development agencies. Most city planning departments and design review boards have implemented community development guidelines and master plans, which require design using specific architectural styles. Building architects have very specific reference materials to assist in this, but landscape architects must scramble and sort through many garden design books, photographs, and magazine clippings to create image boards for agency presentations.

Since landscape architects and designers are not formally educated in architectural style, there are only a few individuals who have obtained the experience to create landscape designs based on architectural style. Even those landscape architects experienced with architectural style have a limited knowledge of the various styles and how those styles can be translated into site element and landscape design.

What you are about to read is intended to fill the present void and impact the profession of landscape architecture in a way no one else has dared to attempt. If you put this resource into your reference library, you will no doubt find use for it in many of your landscape designs.

Introduction

Purpose of This Book

This book is the first of a two-volume set written with the primary purpose of helping professional designers make good decisions about landscape design, decisions that will complement and elevate architectural style. This book may also be used by non-professionals to gain insight into their home's style and how to approach a landscape design that corresponds with that style.

Landscape architects originally worked together with architects to create complementary designs and to develop beautiful communities. This was the vision of Andrew Jackson Downing and Fredrick Law Olmstead. However, the field of landscape architecture has evolved and changed over the years. It seems the profession is continuing to polarize, with one pole using landscape design to gain the greatest return on investment and the opposite pole to emphasize theory and preservation of the environment. Though both of these positions are important, the fundamentals of practical creative landscape design are losing priority, getting lost somewhere in the space between the two poles. It seems the concept of marrying architectural style and landscape design has lost importance. This book is intended to help reestablish the importance of combining landscape and architectural design.

A Guideline for Design

This book represents one designer's opinion for creating landscapes based upon architectural style. That opinion, however, is backed by twenty years of experience in landscape design for retail, commercial, planned development, custom residential, public works, and parks and recreation.

There is no one exact plant palette or one right solution for a design style. Using this book will guide readers toward better design choices and better solutions.

In many cases, sister architectural styles may borrow from each other: an Italian style building may use a Classical plant palette or a Georgian style building may use Early American design elements. It is the designer's discretion to make these decisions.

Architectural Style

The architectural styles in this book are organized roughly chronologically. The book begins with Classical style and ends with the eighth style, Second Empire. These are the styles that were imported into America, primarily in the eastern part of the United States. Most of the styles were inspired in one way or another by European influences. American architectural styles like Classical, Italian, and parts of Georgian were borrowed from Greece, Rome, and Italy. Early American architecture came from England during colonial settlement. French and Second Empire styles were developed by architects who visited France for design inspiration. Gothic and Georgian architecture and architectural elements come from a number of locations in Europe.

Each chapter is dedicated to one major style. There can be many interpretations to the organization of the major styles and the relationships to sub-styles. The major styles are organized and classified in this book for the benefit of the landscape designer.

For more detailed architectural reference, two good companion books to this volume are *A Field Guide to American Houses* by Virginia and Lee McAlester and *American House Styles* by John Milnes Baker.

Designing for Climate Zones

In Coastal Southern California (where I live) the climate makes it possible to build almost any style of architecture. One could find examples of all the styles mentioned in this book within a 100-mile radius in Coastal Southern California.

When designing a building, site, or landscape, it is obviously important to consider the geographic region in which the project resides. The premise of this book assumes the designer is able to discern whether the particular design style and its materials, structures, and plants are available and conducive to that region. Plants given in this book might not be the original plants associated with the architecture style, but are a suitable replacement to complement the style as it was originally intended. A good resource for determining plant adaptability is the *Sunset Western Garden Book*.

In most cases there are many plant substitutions available. For example, the plant palette provided for Early American architecture is based upon Eastern American native plants. If one is designing a landscape in the West, there are many substitutions available which are suitable to the West. In most cases a species of plant can be chosen within the same genus.

Chapter One

CLASSICAL

Roman • Romantic • Romanesque • Greek • Greek Revival • Traditional

HISTORY

Known to many as the Traditional style, the Classical style originated with ancient Greek and Roman architecture. From 900 to 400 B.C., the Greeks were the major influence on architectural style. Under Roman control, the driving force for architectural style evolved from 100 B.C. to 500 A.D.

Since the ancient classical period, there have been some revivals to bring the classical look back. About the time of the American Revolution, the Roman style was revived. Then in the late 1700s to early 1800s, excavations in Greece of old cities like Pompeii began changing the architectural influences in America from Roman to Greek. This was the Greek Revival, which lasted about half of a century. Finally, at the end of the 1800s, the Neo-Classical style emerged, a style that combined both Roman and Greek elements into one.

Though archeological discoveries of the late 1700s took place in Europe, surprisingly, most of the architectural influences came to America and not England. The Bank of Philadelphia was the first building in the United States to be designed with this style. The Americans used Classical design for civic monuments and state capitol buildings. Many new towns in the United States were even named after Greek cities.

Though known for his political contributions, Thomas Jefferson is not always remembered for his works as an architect and landscape architect. Jefferson's contributions came during the transition between the Classical Revival period and the Neo-Classical Period as can be seen by his evolving design for Monticello. Though his final design for Monticello combined brick with the Classical elements (the Georgian style), his first design for Monticello was Greek Revival and influenced much of the architecture following the Revolution. Jefferson's early efforts at garden design have helped define the Classical style landscape.

One of the early manifestations of Classical architecture in America is the Jefferson Memorial in Washington, D.C. The design displays all the elements of Classical architecture, including a tympanum design in the pediment.

The Parthenon in Athens, Greece is one of the remaining examples of classical architecture. *Courtesy of Megan Flanagan.*

ARCHITECTURAL DESIGN

The Classical style is always easy to identify. Greek and Roman styles are very subtly different. The major difference is that the Romans used arches and domes, while this is absent in Greek architecture.

Greek architecture has a very shallow pitched gable roof, with a front facing gable portico. The entries are recessed casement molding and full light windows around a paneled door. The portico is fully columned with a pediment above a wide-banded cornice. On the face of the main structure were long un-pedimented windows with shutters. Square columns were often designed into the façade of the main structure and on its ends. Though the originals were not totally white, revival buildings were constructed in snow white to imply purity (ironically for government buildings).

During the Roman Empire, the availability of materials and labor made it possible for the Caesars to construct many elaborate buildings that would be nearly impossible to build or budget today. Structures like the Coliseum and the Pantheon were constructed from huge, heavy marble blocks and assembled with manpower that would make modern day labor unions cringe.

The biggest problem with the Classical style is its lack of flexibility in form. The architecture originally could only be designed in post and beam construction. Also lacking in Classical design is what Landscape Architect Thomas Church spent his career trying to correct, an absence of human scale. The early engineers used physics to design their buildings, but always erred on the conservative side, yielding edifices with massive structural members. With no building codes, but with inflated egos, Caesars directed their architects to build columns, doorways, and stairs with excessive heights and widths. This resulted in design elements that are over-sized and beyond the human scale. Courtyards and gardens were designed for excess, not for intimate gatherings.

Distinctive Features

- Very formal, symmetrical, over-size scaled.
- Greek is a simple, rectangular structure; Roman adds arches and domes.
- Low-pitched gable roof with pediment supported by columned portico.

Some of the older American universities have used Classical architecture in their buildings like Chapman University in Orange, California, Pomona College, in Claremont, California, and the University of Redlands in Redlands California. *(continued on following page)*

CHAPMAN UNIVERSITY

UNIVERSITY OF REDLANDS
Minds and Hearts

SITE DESIGN

Feature Integration

To integrate the Classical features, design must be formal, with a symmetrical layout of shapes. Site elements are massive and out-of-scale, with simple rectangular geometrics. Common features used to reflect the Classical style into vertical site design are columns, pediments, cornice molding, round arches, and domes. To add interest, details can include fluting, routed molding, spear finials, and Acanthus or fig leaves.

Classical Column Orders

Columns provide the most distinctive feature in integrating Classical style into the landscape. Contained within the Classical style are five basic column designs: Greek Doric, Roman Doric, Tuscan, Ionic, and Corinthian. Columns can be designed into shade covers, water features, fire features, planters, or garden art.

The Agora in Athens, Greece, has Greek Doric columns and a pediment. *Courtesy of Megan Flanagan.*

The columns on the Ancient Forum in Rome, Italy, are Ionic with no fluting. *Courtesy of Megan Flanagan.*

Tuscan columns front this building at Chapman University.

The Pantheon in Rome, Italy, is fronted by non-fluted Corinthian columns and a pediment. *Courtesy of Megan Flanagan.*

The Temple of Olympic Zeus in Athens, Greece, is supported by fluted Corinthian columns. *Courtesy of Megan Flanagan.*

Classical Forms

Materials and Finishes

Classical and Greek Revival architecture was always white. Usually the entire structure was white marble or limestone. Sometimes the style influence came in simply the paint, with white clapboard sidings, but for added color, full-length louvered green or red shutters. This can be translated into primarily white site structures, with black as a secondary color and green or red accents.

The white marble and limestone building materials can be economically replicated with poured-in-place off-white color concrete. The façade and most all exposed wood should be gloss white or off-white. Wrought iron or other steel should be black.

Color Palette

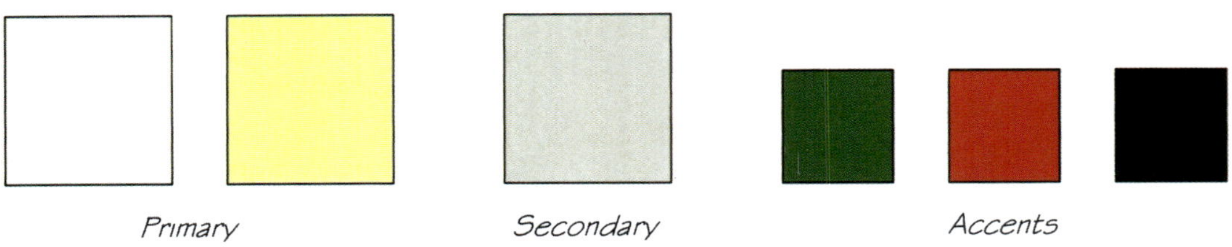

This Roman design shows many elements of the Classical style. *Courtesy of Ted Friebe.*

Though built during the Victorian Era, and having some additional ornamentation, the Abbey in San Diego, California, is a good example of Classical architecture.

Pediment detailing at Caesar's Palace, in Las Vegas, Nevada.

The Getty Villa in Pacific Palisades, California, has an excellent integration of architectural style into site and landscape design.

Paving Design Concepts

Paving

In Classical design, decks and walks are plain, natural color concrete, with rectangular patterns and scoring. Paving would not include masonry construction. Banding could include reverse quarter-round corners to resemble molding. If steps are to be provided, plain, natural color concrete with formed decorative bullnose (rounded step) should be used. Stepping pads should be square, plain, natural color concrete pads.

This street in Rome, Italy shows the use of cobble pavers. Though this is not the original paving for Greek and Roman style, it can be considered Classical paving. *Courtesy of Ted Friebe.*

Classical paving can be simple or have formal decoration. These examples from the Hearst Castle in San Simeon, California, show concrete paving with formal decorative marble inlays.

Wall and Fence Design Concepts

Walls

The Classical style has smooth, white poured-in-place or pre-cast concrete walls, pilasters and balustrades with pre-cast, with formed decorative bullnose caps. If masonry construction is used, it should not be exposed, unless oversized units are used with the intent to replicate the huge Greek and Roman limestone blocks. Pre-cast concrete trim and moldings can be used in detailing to reflect the Greek and Roman pediments and cornices.

Fences

Where Classical wood fencing is desired, white gloss finished lumber posts and pickets with decorative trim and moldings should be used. If metal, fencing should be black wrought iron and gates with spear finials.

These Classical wall designs at Kimberly-Crest House in Redlands, California, and the Hearst Castle show a symmetric layout of rectangular pilasters and balustrades formed in natural color concrete.

Trellises

Trellises are to be constructed from lumber with Classical trim and molding and finished in white. They should be designed to allow open growth of climbing flowering and grape vines.

This model home shows several Classical style site elements: fencing, trellises, and a columned shade structure.

Shade Cover Design Concepts

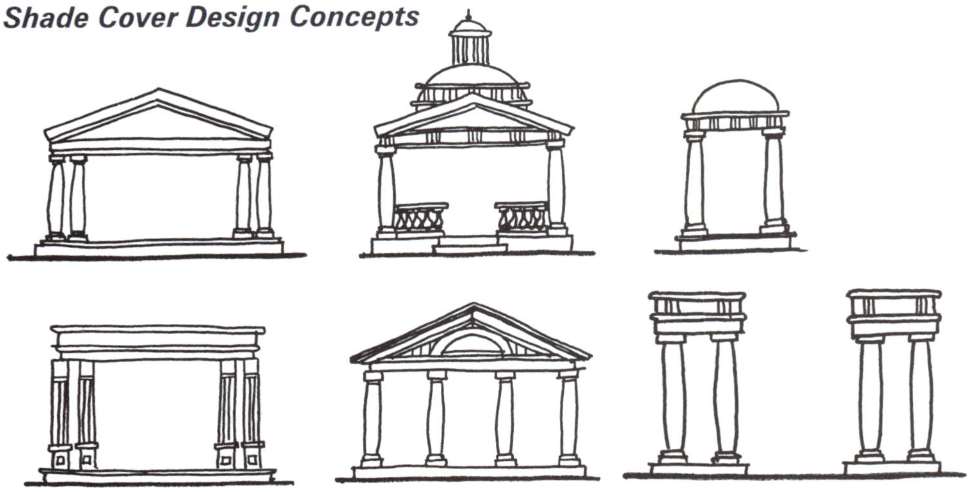

Shade Covers

Probably the easiest site features to design in the Classical style examples are shade structures. To achieve the Classical look, shade covers should be pedimented with a low-pitch roof, supported by Classical columns. Structures might come in the form of a round, arched, or domed pergola.

Classical style shade structures at the Getty Villa in Malibu, California; the Huntington Library in San Marino, California; and at Harveston Lake Park in Temecula, California. *Courtesy of David Ling.*

Likely the best examples of Classical style shade covers are the structures surrounding the Neptune Pool at the Hearst Castle.

This shade cover at Harveston Lake Park is a simple design with classical columns with a canopy of parallel lattice.

A grape arbor designed as a shade cover at the Getty Villa.

Shade cover examples at Caesar's Palace in Las Vegas, Nevada.

Water Feature Design Concepts

This water feature integrates Classical columns and other elements into a water feature. *Courtesy of Megan Flanagan.*

Water Features

The most common Classical water feature would have been (and is) a white rectangular or round basin with Classical style walls. Inside the basin would be simple bowls. Moldings, trim, and other Classical detailing can be added.

Another Classical fountain in Rome. *Courtesy of Ted Friebe.*

The reflecting pools from the Getty Villa are designed with Grecian Classical design forms. The fountain sculptures are also a good example of Classical garden art.

A recreation pool and a wall fountain at Caesar's Palace.

A Classical birdbath at the Getty Villa.

Seating Design Concepts

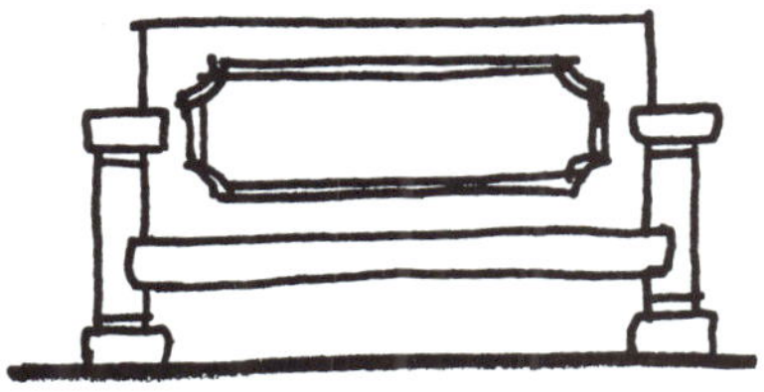

Seating

For a Classical effect, white pre-cast concrete tables and benches with Classical columns for legs or with simple rectangular forms can be used. For rectangular forms, edges should be beveled. An interesting touch can be to use bench legs that resemble papyrus scrolls.

A simple concrete bench at Kimberly-Crest House.

Planter Design Concepts

Planters

In most Classical designs, planters are simple white or off-white pre-cast concrete or plaster pots or urns. Ornamentation with Acanthus or grape leaves is a possibility.

This custom pre-cast concrete urn was created for Kimberly-Crest House before mass production existed.

Garden Art Design Concepts

Garden Art

The common garden art elements found in the Classical style normally include some use of a column or columns to form a pedestal. Whatever the art form, it should have decorative trim and moldings. White plaster or concrete sculptures might include Acanthus leaves, busts, cherubs, women in tunics, or Trojan soldiers.

These statue pedestals of John Smith in Jamestown, Virginia, and of Caesar in Rome both display the Classical style with simple rectangular design, straight moldings, and natural color concrete. *Courtesy of Ted Friebe.*

A white obelisk in Jamestown, Virginia, reaches through a canopy of trees to the blue sky above.

Classical style pedestals, urns, and statuary at Caesar's Palace. *(continued on following page)*

PLANTING DESIGN

The Classical style (the Greek and Roman styles) is the earliest architecture and landscape that is replicated in modern times. The Greek landscape is characterized as formal with many conifers and evergreens. It typically has large leaves and course textures, with subdued flower colors.

The plants commonly used by Greeks in landscape designs can often be seen in buildings and sculptures. Tops of columns are ornamented with Acanthus mollis (Bear's Breach) leaves. Olive branches, grape vines, and, of course, fig leaves are also reflected in art and architecture. In Greek gardens, near water, one might find Weeping Willow or Papyrus. Some Greek landscape designs have an emphasis on vines, as seen in the Seventh Wonder Hanging Gardens of Babylon. Another plant that cannot be forgotten is the Laurel. In the ancient Olympic Games, the reward for the champion was a crown of Laurel leaves.

Plant Palette

Trees

Cedrus deodora	Deodora Cedar
Cedrus atlantica 'glauca'	Blue Atlas Cedar
Citrus sp.	Orange, Lemon, Kumquat
Cupressus sempervirens	Italian Cypress
Ficus benjamina	Weeping Fig
Ficus carica	Edible Fig
Ginkgo biloba	Ginkgo
Laurus nobilis	Grecian Laurel
Ligustrum lucidum	Tree Privet
Olea europea	Olive
Pinus pinea	Italian Stone Pine
Prunus c.'Atropurpurea'	Purple-Leaf Plum
Prunus laurocerasus	English Laurel
Punica granatum	Pomegranate
Phoenix dactilifera	Date Palm
Salix babylonica	Weeping Willow

Shrubs

Acanthus mollis	Bear's Breach
Aralia papyrifera	Rice Paper Plant
Arbutus unedo	Strawberry Tree
Aspidistra elatior	Cast-iron Plant
Agapanthus africanus	Lily-of-the-Nile
Buxus japonica	Japanese Boxwood
Cyperus papyrus	Papyrus
Fatshedera lizei	False Aralia
Fatsia japonica	Japanese Aralia
Gardenia jasminoides	Gardenia
Juniperus sp.	Juniper
Osmanthus fragrans	Sweet Olive
Ligustrum japonicum	Japanese Privet
Liriope muscari	Big Blue Lily Turf
Phormium tenax	New Zealand Flax
Photina fraserii	Fraser's Photinia
Rosmarinus officianalis	Rosemary
Viburnum tinus 'Spring Bouquet'	Spring Bouquet Viburnum

Vines and Espaliers

Beaumontia grandiflora	Easter Lily Vine
Pyracantha	Firethorn
Thymus vulgaria	Thyme
Wisteria sinensis	Chinese Wisteria

Groundcovers

Cissus rhombifolia	Grape Ivy
Hedera helix	English Ivy
Juniperus sp.	Juniper
Pelargonium peltatum	Ivy Geranium
Rhoicissus capensis	Evergreen Grape

Formal courtyard planting designs at the Getty Villa with manicured Boxwood, Oleander, Pomegranate, and Algerian Ivy.

Planting Design Concept

Classical Planting Design

Concept
Simple, formal, symmetrical, manicured, contrasting foliage texture emphasis.

Trees
Large background mass: Prunus laurocerasus (English Laurel)
Columnar background evergreen: Cupressus sempervirens (Italian Cypress)
Picturesque midground canopy: Olea europea (Olive Tree)
Small foreground accent: Citrus sinensis (Dwarf Citrus)

Shrubs
Background hedge: Ligustrum japonicum (Japanese Privet)
Midground hedge: Buxus microphylla japonica (Japanese Boxwood) Midground accent: Cyperus papyrus (Papyrus)
Foreground hedge: Juniperus horizontalis (Spreading Juniper)
Entry and pot accents: Phormium tenax (New Zealand Flax)
Course foreground accent: Acanthus mollis (Bear's Breach)

Vines and Groundcover
Climbing vine: Cissus rhombifolia (Grape Ivy)
Clumping midground: Agapanthus africanus 'Peter Pan' (Dwarf Lily-of-the-Nile)
Trailing foreground: Hedera helix (English Ivy)

The Huntington Library Rose Garden is a formal planting design with solid greens and brilliant color.

The Classical herb garden and surrounding hillside landscape at the Getty Villa have a Classical plant palette with Italian Stone Pine, Italian Cypress, Olive Trees, Citrus, Rosemary, and Lily-of-the-Nile.

Classical planting design at Caesar's Palace with hedges, color, and climbing vines.

Chapter Two

GOTHIC

Gothic • Gothic Revival • Medieval • Medieval Revival

HISTORY

The Gothic style has evolved over such a long time with several revivals and deviations that it is the most difficult style to understand. It began, of course, with the medieval architecture of the Middle Age (between the 6th and 15th centuries A.D.), an era dominated by the designs of grand, fortified castles. In the early Middle Age, the purpose of castles was to serve as defensive structures. Since they housed royalty, it didn't take long for kings to retain architects who would make what was now their home a more attractive place to live. This caused the architecture of castles to become more ornate and elaborate as the centuries passed.

Although the Gothic style was being used for church design since the third century, it was about the 12th century when a transitional emphasis from castle design to church and cathedral design was made. About this time, in England, the Gothic style also became known as the "Christian Style." This was because those dwelling in Gothic style buildings were said to be portraying a "moral life." It is interesting this style had an influence on so many churches and cathedrals, yet the origination of the style occurred in the Medieval Dark Age, when the way of life had no resemblance to what our culture considers "Christian" today.

The earliest medieval castles were constructed for protection against enemy warfare with large masonry walls and little ornamentation or window space. The main distinction in these masses is in their vertical features with battlement towers like Amberley Castle in West Sussex, England. *Courtesy of Todd and Judy Bradstreet.*

Later castle architecture became less defensive and took on more ornamentation. This castle not only has battlements, but decorative colored masonry with quoin-like corners, cresting, multiple windows, and pinnacle chimneys. *Courtesy of Todd and Judy Bradstreet.*

The Gothic style also had a period of influence on residential design. The first "Gothic Revival" for residential design actually started in England in 1749 with Sir Horace Walpole, who remodeled his own home, Strawberry Hill, borrowing several of the Gothic elements like pointed arches and simulated battlements.

In America, interest in Classical architecture was beginning to waiver in the 1830s and the Gothic Revival soon arrived. It was the style that was the transition into the famous Victorian Period that would inspire architects to create several unforgettable styles of architecture.

Though castles started integrating architectural features like lancet arched windows with ornamentation and other elements like dentils and crosses, their primary purpose was to serve as a defensive fortress with strong vertical walls as seen at Arundel Castle in West Sussex, England. *Courtesy of Todd and Judy Bradstreet.*

As medieval design transformed into Gothic Architecture, castle features appeared in European churches and estates. St. Peter's Church in Wisborough Green, England, retains the primary castle elements with masonry construction and a vertical emphasis. Other carry-overs are battlement cresting, lancet windows, and masonry pinnacles. An added window feature that became distinctive to residential Gothic style is diamond panel glass. *Courtesy of Todd and Judy Bradstreet.*

Architectural Design

Traditional castle-influenced Gothic architecture is always easy to identify: vertical construction with large-unit dark-gray masonry. Though there was some wood-framed construction in Gothic church design, most of the remaining examples are from materials able to survive over the centuries.

Virtually every castle and cathedral in Europe and America displays the traditional elements common to Gothic architecture to one degree or another: massive units, castellations, battlements, towers, and pointed arches. Different with cathedral design, however, is the use of white instead of gray. Also common to cathedral design is an extensive use of ornamentation. The most elaborate buildings have numerous decorative features, emphasizing the vertical, in symmetrical patterns like pointed parapets, spires, pinnacles, or chimneystacks.

The Gothic Revival introduced extravagant designs as architects used the medieval features to design grand cathedrals; no longer defensive buildings, they were works of art. The Notre Dame Cathedral in Paris, France is one of the most famous examples of this style. By the way, the man in the photo is not blind; he is my brother, Todd. *Courtesy of Judy Bradstreet.*

Cathedrals like Westminster Abbey, in London, England, show the level of extravagant ornamentation a Gothic design can have. *Courtesy of Todd and Judy Bradstreet.*

The Gothic Revival brought a very different look to residential architectural design. Normally, it is wood frame construction with clapboard siding, board and batten siding, or a brick façade. The architecture has a steep gable roof, usually with cross gables, and with the most distinguishable feature, decorative scrolling (vergeboards), tucked under the eaves. In the later designs, vergeboards were replaced with decorative trusses. Most residential Gothic buildings have a one-story porch with decorative posts and pointed arches (lancets) set in the center of a symmetrical structure. Always present is the trademark pointed arch either for the door or a prominent window that typically protrudes upward into the gable or a parapet.

The door is normally recessed into a cross gable side of the building with a balcony above. Ornamentations can occur on windows, doors, roof connections, and porches. Other common features are clay chimney pots, gable dormers, patterned block masonry, diamond partition windows, and cast iron cresting and balcony rails.

Distinctive Features (Castles and Cathedrals)

- Extreme vertical emphasis
- Symmetrical structure in most cases
- Large-unit masonry construction
- Use of castellations, battlements, towers, and pointed arches.
- Symmetrical patterns of pointed parapets, spires, pinnacles, or chimney stacks

Distinctive Features (Residential Gothic Revival)

- Symmetrical structure
- Pointed parapet roof with vergeboard eaves
- Pointed arches, doors, and diamond-pane windows

During the eighteenth and nineteenth centuries, America accepted the Gothic Revival movement as churches and cathedrals were built throughout the country. These churches are from the southern California cities of Pomona, Los Angeles, and Pasadena. *(continued on following two pages)*

SITE DESIGN

Feature Integration

The integration of the Gothic style into site design starts with a symmetrical layout of shapes, primarily square vertical forms. Whether castle, cathedral, or residence, vertical design features and pointed arches must be included. Other ways to implement the Gothic style are to include patterned masonry, diamond shape detailing, or decorative woodwork scrolling. For site elements where vertical emphasis can be implemented, the use of battlements, castellations, towers, multiple parapets, spires, and pinnacles will create the Gothic appeal.

Gothic Forms

Materials and Finishes

Unless an unlimited budget is available or materials can't be harvested locally, the cost and transportation of large cut stone would exclude traditional construction methods from site design. To replicate traditional Gothic design with modern available materials, it is best to use concrete masonry unit (CMU) construction with a stone facade. Façade materials for castle-like design should be large blocks of dark gray cut stone in simple bond courses. For cathedrals, budgets may allow use of limestone, but if not, white large cut stone blocks can be used.

For Gothic Revival construction, materials are wood construction with cool-color finished vertical siding and white decorative wood scrolling for ornamentation. If steel is to be used; it should have a black finish.

Color Palette

A rare modern day use of Gothic architectural design is this winery in Napa Valley, California. *Courtesy of Darin Farnworth.*

During the Gothic Revival, homes were inspired by the movement, but since lumber was the primary material of choice, some additional design features emerged. This residence shows the board and batten siding, and archway cresting prevalent to residential Gothic architecture.

Residential Gothic architecture normally includes archway cresting called "vergeboards," as shown here at the Queen Victorian Bed and Breakfast in Cape May, New Jersey. *Courtesy of the Queen Victorian Inn.*

Paving Design Concepts

Paving

Gothic style paving should be designed with a symmetrical layout of rectangular forms, but with an irregular inset of materials. Design can be with concrete, rectangular cut stone, or both. If with two materials, the secondary material can be used for straight banding. Steps should be simple cut stone or formed concrete, creating either a non-bullnose or right angle bullnose riser. Stepping pads should be squares of rectangular concrete or large, gray cut stone.

Typical Gothic paving includes large rectangular cobble pavers and stepping stones.

Wall and Fence Design Concepts

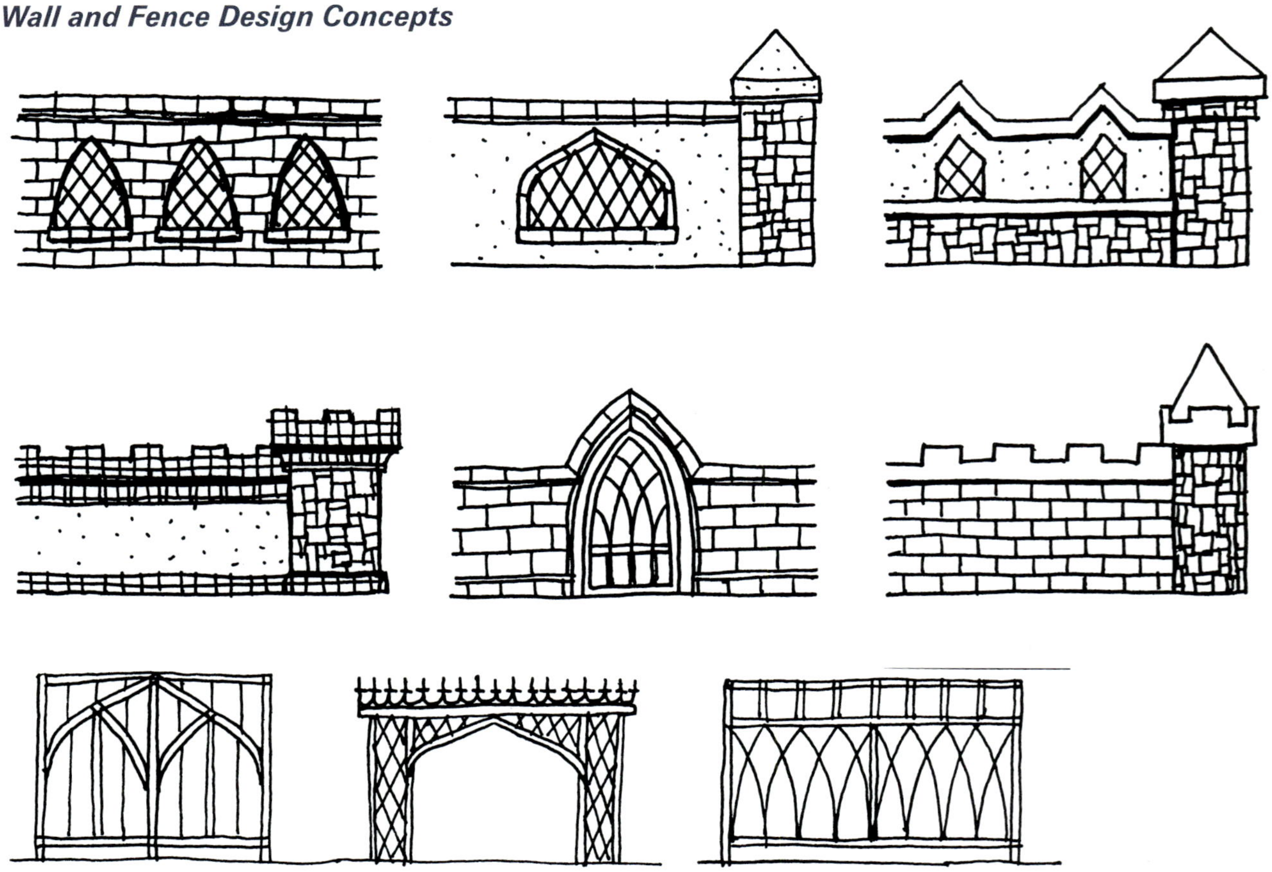

Walls

For walls to resemble traditional Gothic architecture, they should have a large cut stone façade in either running bond or irregular courses. If caps are used, there is an opportunity to introduce some castle-like Gothic features with use of battlement and castellation forms. Simple caps can be stone or formed, pointed concrete. The use of pilasters also creates opportunity for use of Gothic features. Pointed turrets, battlements, and even pinnacles can be used.

In the Gothic style, there are some features easily translated from architecture to fence design. The use of spears atop of wrought iron pickets follows medieval weaponry. In addition, the use of pinnacles and other finials for post tops keep with the style. Gateways should have pointed arches.

For wood fencing, Gothic revival elements can be used, like board and batten siding with vergeboard detailing beneath the cap.

This reconstruction of a Medieval castle shows heavy wall construction for Gothic style with large, rectangular, semi-irregular masonry units. *Courtesy of Tammi Strasen.*

Trellis Design Concepts

Trellises

As with fencing, trellises can reflect Gothic design through the use of black wrought iron. With pointed arches, whether angled or curved, some interesting ideas can be developed using spears and finals.

Shade Cover Design Concepts

Shade Covers

It wouldn't make much sense to design a shade cover to resemble a castle using all masonry construction. However, it is possible to design a structure with stone pilasters and a wood cover. Whether with pilasters or wood posts, a wood cover can easily be designed for the Gothic style with the use of a steep, pointed roof and finials. If walls appear on the sides, they should be board and batten. It is also possible to include decorative vergeboarding for roof edges.

A good design for a Gothic gazebo would have vertical emphasis. This design at the Nixon Library and Birthplace also has a domed top with a pointed final, creating a lancet-like appearance.

Water Feature Design Concepts

Water Features

The stone materials indicative to the Gothic style are to be implemented in water feature design. Water features are to be simple and formal.

Fire Feature Design Concepts

Fire Features

Designs for fireplaces and barbeques can display the Gothic style with the use of cut stone. The natural vertical design of fireplaces makes them easy to include Gothic features like pointed parapets and arches, pinnacles, and smoke stacks.

Seating Design Concepts

Seating

Seating for Gothic style can be designed with stone, steel, or wood using any of the variety of materials or distinctive features, whether it be rectangular stone, vertical steel, board and batten siding, or vergeboards.

Planter Design Concepts

Planters

Most planters for the Gothic style would be built-in and not pots. Planters would be cut stone with stone or concrete caps.

Black wrought iron can be used to create a Gothic look for fencing and planter barrier edging.

The Smithsonian Institute Museum in Washington D.C. is an example of Gothic architecture with a complementary paving, wall, and planting design. Like the building, the garden has a formal, symmetrical layout of hedges and groundcovers. In plan view, the hedges resemble diamond pane windows with diagonal rows framed by a rectangular form.

PLANTING DESIGN

The Gothic landscape design is normally formal and symmetrical, but can be semi-formal. The Gothic style is the antithesis of the Victorian planting design style. Like its architecture, the Gothic plant palette is dark, hard, coarse, and sharp. Just as the Victorian garden is inviting, the Gothic garden is forbidding. There are few flowers and little contrast of foliage color. As with the building edges, plant forms are sharp, with thorns and serrated leaves. The Gothic style has hedges similar to the Victorian, but instead of flowering shrubs for accents, plain, non-contrasting greens are prevalent. The overall scale of the Gothic landscape is large and inhuman.

The most distinct garden feature that emerged from the Gothic period is the hedge maze. Most true Gothic gardens include a hedge maze with a creative design pattern.

A Gothic landscape might be designed with a somewhat "defensive" effect like the castles of the Medieval Age. This can be achieved with thorny plant material like roses and tight corridors. Though this photo shows a beautiful garden design, the space still tells the visitor, "Proceed with caution."

Plant Palette

Trees

Acacia baileyana	Bailey Acacia
Acer rubrum	Red Maple
Acer saccharum	Sugar Maple
Ceratonia siliqua	Carob Tree
Cinnamomum camphora	Camphor Tree
Cedrus deodora	Deodora Cedar
Citrus sp.	Orange, Lemon
Cupressus macrocarpa	Monterey Cypress
Dizygotheca elegantissima	ncn
Ficus sp.	Ornamental Fig
Juniperus torulosa	Twisted Juniper
Liquidambar styraciflua	American Sweet Gum
Magnolia grandiflora	Southern Magnolia
Pinus pinea	Italian Stone Pine
Pinus radiata	Monterey Pine
Platanus occidentalis	American Sycamore
Prunus c. 'Atropurpurea'	Purple-leaf Plum
Quercus kellogii	Valley Oak

Shrubs

Abelia grandiflora	Glossy Abelia
Arbutus unedo	Strawberry Tree
Berberis thunbergii	Barberry
Buxus microphylla	Japanese Boxwood
Cocculus laurifolius	ncn
Cotoneaster sp.	Cotoneaster
Dietes iridioides	African Iris
Euonymous sp.	Euonymous
Grevillea 'Noellii'	Noel's Grevillea
Ilex sp.	Holly
Juniperus sp.	Juniper
Ligustrum japonicum	Japanese Privet
Myrsine africana	African Boxwood
Osmanthus fragrans	Sweet Olive
Pittosporum tobira	Mock Orange
Rosa sp.	Rose
Sansevieria trifasciata	Mother-In-Law's Tongue
Syzygium paniculatum	Australian Brush Cherry
Viburnum sp.	Viburnum

Vines and Espaliers

Convolvulus cneorum	Bush Morning Glory
Distictis buccinatoria	Blood-Red Trumpet Vine
Parthenocissus tricuspidata	Boston Ivy
Pyracantha sp.	Firethorn
Rosa sp.	Rose
Vaccinium	Huckleberry

Groundcovers

Hedera canariensis	Algerian Ivy

Planting Design Concept

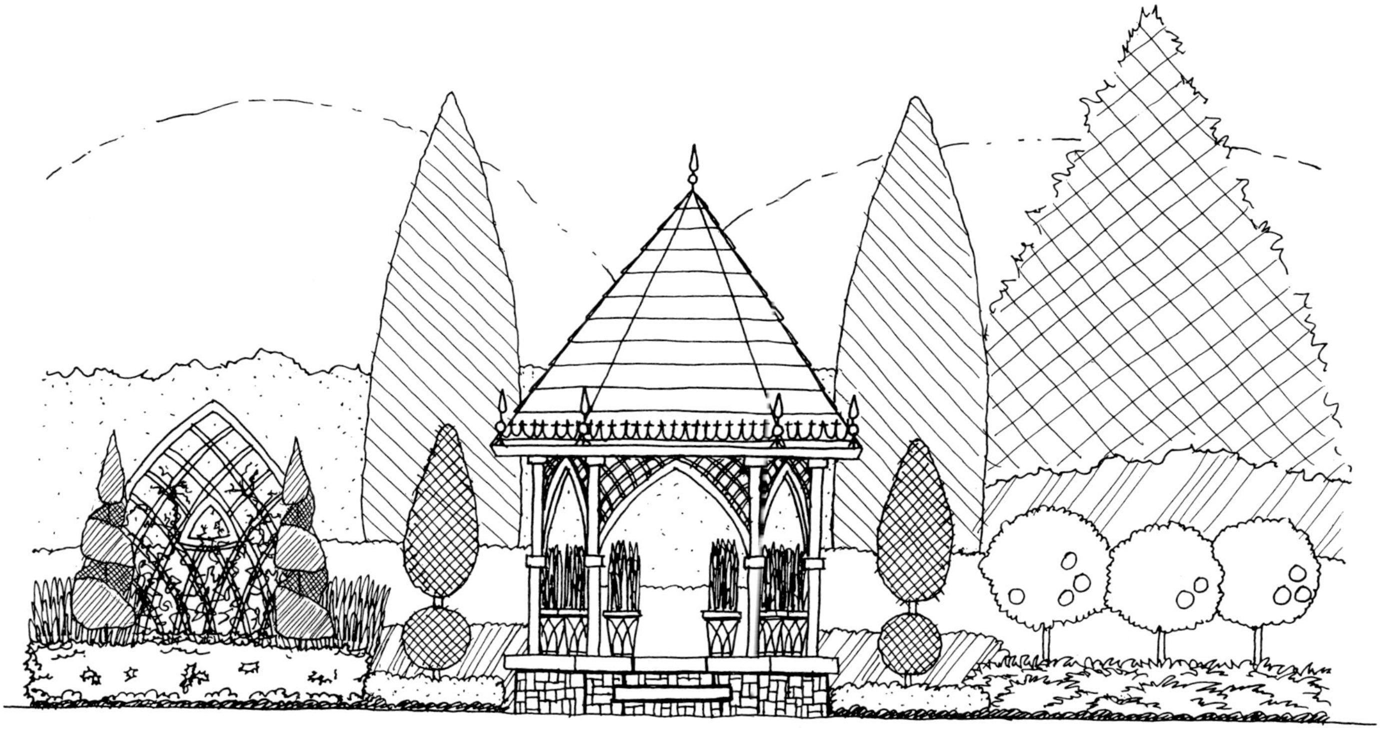

Gothic Planting Design

Concept
Simple, formal or semi-formal, symmetrical, manicured, vertical design emphasis.

Trees
Large background mass: Ceratonia siliqua (Carob Tree)
Columnar background evergreen: Cupressus sempervirens (Italian Cypress)
Midground vertical accent: Cedrus deodora (Deodora Cedar)
Small foreground accent: Citrus sinensis (Dwarf Citrus)

Shrubs
Background mass: Cotoneaster lacteus (Parney Cotoneaster)
Midground hedge: Euonymous fortunei (Euonymous)
Midground accent: Dietes iridioides (Fortnight Lily)
Midground topiary: Syzigium paniculatum (Australian Brush Cherry)
Midground vertical accent: Juniperus chinensis (Corkscrew Juniper)
Foreground hedge: Ilex vomitoria (Dwarf Yaupon)
Entry and pot accents: Sansevieria trifasciata (Mother-In-Law's Tongue)
Course foreground accent: Berberis thunbergii (Barberry)

Vines and Groundcover
Espalier: Pyracantha sp. (Firethorn)
Trailing foreground: Grevillea 'Noellii' (Noel's Grevillea)

Chapter Three

EARLY AMERICAN

Post-Medieval English • Early English • Early English Colonial • Colonial English • Early Colonial • Colonial • Early Colonial Revival • Colonial Revival • Dutch Colonial

HISTORY

It may seem unnecessary to include Early American architectural style in this book, since the basic structural framing design wouldn't comply with modern building codes. However, this style needs to be included to better understand the history of American architecture, because this style is the predecessor of many other styles like American Farm (Ranch), Cape Cod, Cabin, and Craftsman.

The Early American style is the result of limited ability for English settlers to convert raw materials into construction materials and to find qualified tradesmen, combined with difficult climactic conditions. These constraints were the biggest factors in architectural design for the first colonies. The product of these constraints was the "Saltbox" design, which was a crude wood-framed box structure.

The Saltbox is a simple, all-lumber structure with a large masonry chimney. These replicas in Yorktown, Virginia, show the simplicity of design. The Saltbox was the earliest architectural style in America. With its origins based in simplicity, it was the predecessor to many other architectural styles like Ranch, Cape Cod, and Cabin. Native materials were harvested and used for lumber and masonry.

ARCHITECTURAL DESIGN

The Early American design is one of the most extreme simplicity. In the North, the Saltboxes were constructed with large timbers and were normally two-story structures. The primary features for the northern Saltboxes were a steep side-gable, a wood shingle roof, and clapboard siding. The doors were simple vertical planks in two sections (Dutch doors). Because glass had to be imported from England, it was used sparingly. Rather than having large pieces of glass with few mullions, the windows were small with many pieces of small diamond-shaped glass partitions. Saltboxes also had overscaled, enormous brick or stone chimneys. The gable roofs had little or no overhang and end gables were fasciated, with no exposed rafters.

In the South, where lime was more available, the Saltboxes were built using brick. Other than the materials and the fact that many of the southern structures were one-story, most of the features were the same as in the North.

Distinctive Features
- Steep side-gable, wood shingle roof
- Enormous brick or stone chimney, sometimes dual
- Clapboard siding with small, diamond partitioned casement windows.

Site Design

Feature Integration

There are few unique forms that can be extrapolated from the Saltbox to the landscape. Most style integration would need to be made through the use of complementary materials. The overall form (or absence of) is simple, boxy geometrics. The use of multiple parallel horizontal lines can mimic clapboard siding. Probably the only real distinctive feature that can be repeated is diamond-shaped accents to resemble the Saltbox windows.

If is wasn't possible to cut lumber because of tools or time, colonists used hewn logs.

As more settlers came to America, more features were added to the Saltbox for interest. These structures from the Granary at Mount Vernon, Home of George Washington in Virginia show round structures and the beginnings of half-timbering.

Early American Forms

Materials and Finishes

The basic construction of the Early American style is large exposed rough-sawn timbers with a simple façade design of wood siding with a natural, weathered or unfinished look. Hardscape materials used are common brick or dry stacked river rock stone. The overall look, of course, is rough and unfinished. Metal can be used sparingly. If it is used, it should be finished in black. No ornamentation is used in this style. Occasionally half-timbering was used, creating a different façade finish.

Colonists realized an all-lumber structure had drafts because of the gaps in the siding. They borrowed the technique of half-timbering from the French and English to fill the gaps.

Building a lumber structure without steel ties required ingenuity. This photo shows the use of mortise and tenon connections for posts and beams.

Color Palette

Paving Design Concepts

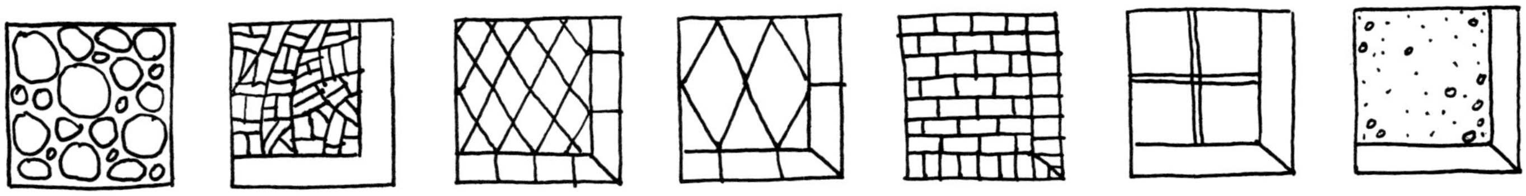

Paving

The layout of paving for Early American design is purely for function, with no need for aesthetics. Walkways are simple and informal. A meandering path would achieve the natural look of the Colonial times. They can be constructed from decomposed granite or plain, natural color concrete. If masonry is to be used, it should be used sparingly, possibly just as irregular banding. Where steps are used, the simplicity can be shown with natural color concrete and a radiused riser, no cantilever. If desired, used brick can be used for steps, but with concrete landings. Step pads should be square, plain, natural color concrete.

Wall Design Concepts

Walls

To design walls in the Early American style, it doesn't require much creativity. Simple dry-stacked river rock or used brick to resemble the large Saltbox chimneys can be used. Dry-stacked rock can be battered or placed vertically. If used brick is employed, it should be in a simple running bond pattern or in a non-uniform pattern. Grout joints should be extruded, not tooled for the rustic effect. A combination of both rock and brick materials is also a possibility. Simplicity means a sparing use of pilasters.

Fencing Design Concepts

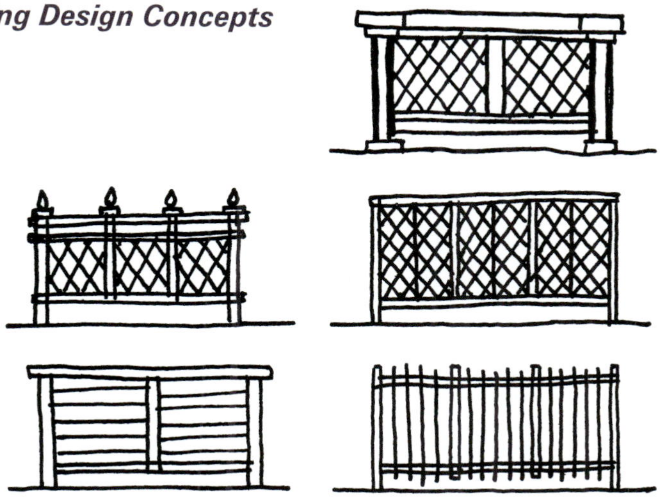

Fences

If wood fencing is to be used, it should be milled horizontal wood siding or vertical wood plank with a weathered finish. More commonly, the settlers used split lumber and even woven branches to quickly construct boundaries to their land. Metal fencing gives an opportunity to integrate diamond-paned Saltbox window forms. Diamond patterns can be designed into black wrought iron.

The farming life of early settlers necessitated the development of boundary fencing. These examples from Yorktown and Mount Vernon were developed for this purpose. Some of these simple designs are still used by farmers and ranchers today. *(continued on following two pages)*

The early Americans had to use the materials that were available to build barrier fencings for protection, like this replica in Jamestown, Virginia.

Trellis Design Concepts

Trellises

As with fencing, trellises should be simple wood construction, created using woven branches. The diamond pane pattern can also be used for trellises if wrought iron is desired.

If settlers built arbor structures, they probably would have looked like this one at Monticello, Home of Thomas Jefferson in Virginia.

Shade Cover Design Concepts

Shade Covers

The Early American Saltbox design can be easily translated into shade cover design with its gable wood shingle roof. This style is simple, so pilasters should not be used. The posts and beams should be squared, undressed lumber, with the same for bracing and trusses. If possible, construction using mortise and tenon would follow traditional Early American design. If not possible, exposed metal ties should be used sparingly and with a rustic quality. Carriage bolts and nails would appear more realistic than hex-head bolts.

These shade structure and barn designs from Mount Vernon, Yorktown, and Jamestown are examples of simple lumber structures from the Early American Era.

Water Feature Design Concepts

Water Features

The true Early American water feature would be a natural river rock stream. It is also possible to make a simple feature with just a river-rock walled basin, well, or birdbath. Fountains can be a combination of brick and river rock.

Fire Feature Design Concepts

Fire Features

The Saltbox chimney provides an opportunity to translate an element into the landscape. An informal design with irregularly placed brick or dry stacked stone for fireplaces, barbeques, and fire pits can resemble the Early American chimneys.

Seating Design Concepts

Seating

Permanent seating for this style can be just a rectangular block of dry-stacked rock. Portable seating can be simple large timber and plank wood tables and benches. The original designs probably also included raw lumber and woven branches, which would also be appropriate.

Early American site furnishings would be very simple. This table is probably one of the more elaborate designs used by the colonists.

Planters

Early American planters are simple dry-stacked rock walls or simple running bond brick. Pots might be hand-carved logs.

Garden Art

Hand-carved statuary, woven baskets, and ironwork are among the possibilities for garden art.

Early American planting design choices were either the natural landscape or an edible garden. The common native trees are Maple, Pine, Dogwood, and Redbud.

PLANTING DESIGN

The Early American planting design style is a combination of native eastern plants and farmed plants used for their edible or floral value. The overall design is an informal layout, predominantly designed with fruit and flowers available for convenience of garden selection and picking. These are complemented by a few showy ornamentals.

Plant Palette

Trees

Acer palmatum	Japanese Maple
Acer rubrum	Red Maple
Acer saccharum	Sugar Maple
Aesculus hippocastanum	Horse Chestnut
Amelanchier canadensis	Serviceberry
Carya lacinosa	Shellbark Hickory
Carya ovata	Shagbark Hickory
Catalpa bignoides	Southern Catalpa
Cedrus deodora	Deodora Cedar
Cedrus atlantica 'glauca'	Blue Atlas Cedar
Cercis canadensis	Eastern Redbud
Chionanthus virginicus	Fringe Tree
Cornus florida	Flowering Dogwood
Crataegus laevigata	English Hawthorn
Fraxinus americana	White Ash
Ginkgo biloba	Ginkgo
Itea virginica	Virginia Sweetspire
Ilex opaca	American Holly
Juglans nigra	Black Walnut
Juniperus virginiana	Eastern Red Cedar
Lagerstroemia indica	Crape Myrtle
Liriodendrun tulipfera	Tulip Tree
Magnolia grandiflora	Southern Magnolia
Malus coronaria	Wild Crabapple
Melia azedarach	Chinaberry
Ostrya virginiana	American Hornbeam
Pyrus calleryana	Ornamental Pear
Platanus acerifolia	London Plane Tree
Pinus strobes	White pine
Pinus virginiana	Virginia Pine
Prunus sp.	Cherry and Plum
Punica granatum	Pomegranate
Quercus nigra	Water Oak
Quercus velutina	Black Oak
Quercus virginiana	Live Oak
Robinia pseudoacacia	Black Locust
Salix sp.	Willow
Thuja occidentalis	American Arborvitae
Tilia americana	American Linden
Ulmus americana	American Elm

Shrubs

Abelia grandiflora	Abelia
Amelanchier sp.	Serviceberry
Azalea indica	Southern Azalea
Berberis thunbergii	Thornberry
Buxus sempervirens	Boxwood
Camellia sp.	Camellia
Cotoneaster sp.	Cotoneaster
Eleagnus pungens	Silverberry
Euonymous atropurpureus	Burning Bush
Garrya elliptica	Silktassel
Gevillea 'Noellii'	Noel's Grevillea
Ilex sp.	Holly
Juniperus sp.	Juniper
Myrtus communis	Common Myrtle
Philadelphus sp.	Mock Orange
Photinia fraserii	Red Top Photina
Rosa sp.	Rose
Syringa vulgaris	Common Lilac
Taxus baccata	English Yew
Viburnum sp.	Viburnum

Vines and Espaliers

Parthenocissus tricuspidata	Boston Ivy
Wisteria sinensis	Chinese Wisteria

Groundcover

Turf	
Alcea rosea	Hollyhock
Iris sp.	Iris
Thymus vulgaria	Thyme
Rosmarinus officinalis	Rosemary

Annuals (See recommended further readings)

Planting Design Concept

Early American Planting Design

Concept
Simple, informal, asymmetrical, natural massings.

Trees
Large background mass: Ilex opaca (American Holly) and Cratageus sp. (Hawthorn)
Background vertical evergreen: Pinus virginiana (Virginia Pine) and Juniperus virginiana (Eastern Red Cedar)
Deciduous upright background: Acer rubrum (Red Maple) and Quercus virginiana (Virginia Oak)
Flowering midground canopy: Cornus florida (Flowering Dogwood), Melia azedarach (Chinaberry), and Cercis canadensis (Eastern Redbud)
Small foreground accent: Prunus sp. (Plum and Cherry Tree)

Shrubs
Background mass: Viburnum sp. (Viburnum)
Midground mass: Philadelphus sp. (Mock Orange) and Ilex sp. (Holly)
Midground accent: Amelanchier sp. (Serviceberry) and Syringa sp. (Lilac)
Foreground mass: Euonymous atropurpureus (Burning Bush)
Annual accent: Alcea rosea (Hollyhock)
Foreground accent: Iris sp. (Iris)

Groundcover
Spreading mass: Juniperus horizontalis (Spreading Juniper)
Low spreading mass: Thymus vulgaria (Thyme) and Rosmarinus officinalis (Rosemary)

Common native Early American shrubs are Dogwood, Holly, and Lilac.

Chapter Four

GEORGIAN

Jacobean • Georgian • New England • Middle Atlantic • South • Adam • Federal • Jeffersonian • Bostonian • Traditional • Plantation

HISTORY

There are a number of related styles that emerged between the Revolutionary War and the Civil War. For simplicity, we will refer to the architecture of this era as the Georgian style.

The Georgian style actually occurred before the Greek Revival style, though it attempted to incorporate many elements of the Greek style. In the 1830s, discoveries from ancient Rome inspired architects to begin the Greek Revival style. Prior to that period, architects had to rely on other sources for their incorporation of Greek elements into the Georgian style.

As American settlers gained wealth, architectural design became more important and more elaborate. An emphasis on English etiquette and a search for civility and order created a style that was very formal and had a clean appearance.

Independence Hall in Buena Park, California, a replica of the original Independence Hall, is the quintessential example of Georgian architecture with a red brick façade and white trim.

ARCHITECTURAL DESIGN

It is usually easy to identify a Georgian style building. This style combines the forms and features of the Classical style with either red brick or wood siding.

The Georgian style typically has a medium-steep gable or sometimes hipped or gambrel roof. The pitch of the roof is enough to allow for the use of dormers. In the mid-1800s, glass became more readily available since it could be fabricated in the United States. This made it possible to create larger (and taller) windows. Most windows from this style were 6 over 6, with at least one of the floor's windows pedimented. The top-lighted front doors were paneled with casement molding and pediments. Some of the architecture even incorporated the Greek columned porticos.

A later divergence from the Georgian was the Federal. The Federal introduced the Roman Palladian by using a front gable (door on the end side of the gable) for placement of a dramatic building entry. Elaborate door and façade trim with fully lighted doors were common. It was also common to find full-height entries and full façade porches fronted with Doric columns. Wrought iron detailing was sometimes used.

Distinctive Features

- Symmetrical, geometric forms
- Use of Classical elements: columns, pediments, trim, and molding
- Use of red brick or clapboard siding, tall windows with shutters

One of the first architects of America, Thomas Jefferson designed Monticello, his home in Virginia, with Classical elements like columns and molding combined with the Early American material of brick. This eventually became Georgian style. Also a landscape architect, Jefferson integrated the Georgian style into site and landscape design.

The indigenous architecture of New England is the Georgian style, as can be seen in this building at the College of William and Mary in Williamsburg, Virginia. Notice the brick façade with tall windows and dormers.

Site Design

Feature Integration

The Georgian style is very formal, with nearly every design feature in a symmetrical layout. Shapes and elements have multiple repetitions. Forms have simple geometrics, mostly rectangles.

The clearest translation of the Georgian style into the landscape is the use of common red brick combined with white Classical columns, pediments, cornice molding, or round arches. Sometimes this can be as easy as using red brick with formed concrete bases and caps.

Various Georgian style residences throughout America, each with columned and pedimented entries, formal landscape layout and hedging, and brickwork. *(continued on following 5 pages)*

843

Georgian Forms

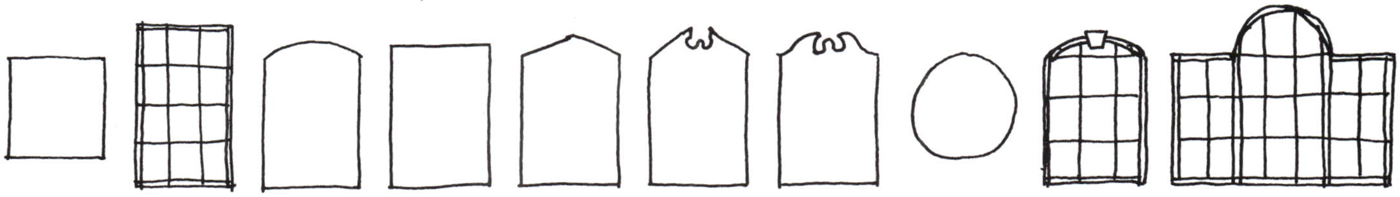

Georgian Pediment Styles

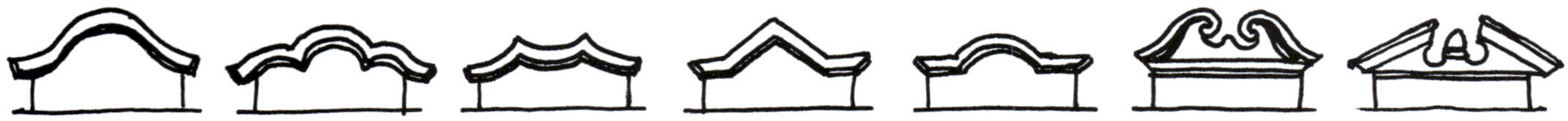

Materials and Finishes

The most common materials for the Georgian style are red brick with struck grout joints and natural color concrete. For wood site elements, white gloss painted lumber in horizontal patterns and white painted decorative moldings and trim is to be used. Where color accents are needed, dark green or crimson red follows the Georgian style. If steel is to be used, it should be black wrought iron.

Color Palette

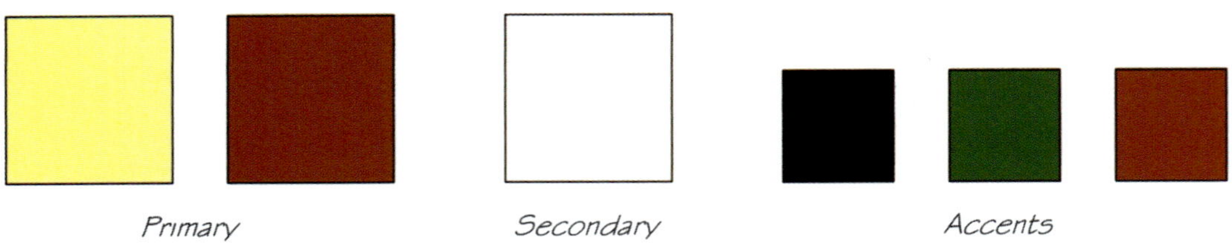

Paving Design Concepts

Paving

As with all Georgian style design, paving should be provided in geometric symmetrical and formal patterns. Georgian style walkways and decks should be a combination of brick and concrete. Concrete is to be plain natural color, with rectangular patterns and scoring. Masonry should be common red brick pavers for banding and field expanses. If entire walkways are not brick, accent areas like building entries should be brick fields. Field patterns can be basket weave, running bond, or herringbone. Steps can be cantilevered common or bullnose red brick. Step pads can be plain natural color concrete squares or fields of brick with perimeter banding.

Brick paving at Monticello and in an English garden.

Brick steps and cheek walls rise to meet the main residence, also at Monticello.

Wall Design Concepts

Walls

A Georgian style wall can be either all brick or a combination of brick and concrete. Wall and pilaster veneer designs have red brick veneer in running bond or decorative patterns. For an all masonry wall or pilaster, bases and caps can be red common or bullnose brick. For a combination, bases and caps can be formed natural color concrete or white decorative pre-cast molding.

Brick wall and white wood picket fencing at Mount Vernon and Monticello.

Fence Design Concepts

Fences

Where steel fencing is used, it should be black wrought iron with ornamentation. Where simplicity is indicative of the Early American style, the Georgian allows for decorative detailing at post, rail, and picket as long as it remains consistent with the formal look. For wood fencing and gates, the Georgian has wood slat or decorative geometric picket patterns and finials with a white gloss lacquer finish.

Brick walls and pilasters with formed concrete caps with black wrought fencing from Stevens House in Tustin, California; Pomona College in Claremont, California; Monticello; and Colonial Jamestown.
(continued on following two pages)

Trellis Design Concepts

Trellises

As with all other styles, the trellises follow the fencing design. Placement of trellises is important so that the Georgian formality is conveyed. As with fencing, trellises are to be black wrought iron or white gloss finished lumber.

A vine trellis in the garden at Mount Vernon.

Shade Cover Design Concepts

Shade Covers

If the cover for an overhead is lattice, it can be flat with crown molding. A solid cover could follow the Classical style, with a low-pitch pediment.

The shade cover supports for the Georgian style can be a variety of designs. Supports can be full columns, pilasters with posts, or full posts. Columns can be Classical or red brick with brick or concrete bases and caps. Pilasters can be the same with square posts. Or if full posts are used they are to be in the Classical white gloss lumber. Posts should have ornamentation with routing and can have plant-ons, trim, and surrounds.

Some potential gazebo inspirations from Mount Vernon and Monticello. The red-roof structure is actually an outhouse, possibly the most beautiful ever designed.

Water Feature Design Concepts

Water Features

The materials, elements, and forms available in the Georgian style offer many opportunities for designing water features. Reflecting pools, fountains, and birdbaths can be designed and sited consistent with the formality of the Georgian style. The most likely design for water features would be similar to Classical style with natural formed concrete in simple geometric forms, but with formed bullnose coping. Bowls and wall fountains can be constructed from red brick with pre-cast concrete caps, trim, and moldings.

Fire Feature Design Concepts

Fire Features

As with the Early American style, the use of brick in the Georgian style enables the designer to create traditional fireplaces for outdoor fire features. The Early American fireplaces can be used or brick with touches of the Classical elements for bases, caps, and moldings can be added to create the Georgian style. It would be common to find formed pre-cast concrete for hearths and mantles. Fire pits and barbeques are to be designed with common red brick veneer. Designers should keep in mind, fire features should have natural color concrete for trim, and not white, so smoke residue is less visible.

This fireplace at Monticello demonstrates the simplicity of Early American brickwork integrated into the Georgian style.

Seating Design Concepts

Seating

Permanent Georgian seat walls are designed with red brick veneer and can have either brick or natural color pre-cast or formed concrete caps. Portable seating should be constructed from lumber with white gloss finish over routed edges on trim and post surrounds or may be unfinished milled lumber. The use of pediment forms provides some opportunity to design some interesting backrests for benches.

A brick seat wall at the College of William and Mary.

Simple bench seating in the Georgian landscape.

Planters

Permanent Georgian style planters are brick running bond veneer or brick and concrete trim combinations. Pots can be decorative white plaster or natural color concrete urns. Symmetry of pot layout is important: even numbers of pots for lined walkways and building frontages.

Garden Art

The Georgian Era is a specific time in America that can be reflected in the landscape with period garden art. Since the era took place between the Revolutionary and Civil wars, a good opportunity for garden statuary can be anything that relates to historical American warfare. Cannons, obelisks, and statues of historical figures are a few examples.

Some potential inspirations for garden art design. Cannons are not recommended for children without adult supervision.

Planting Design

The Georgian style plant palette is rooted in the Classical style, but has undergone a number of changes, caused by a number of cultural and environmental factors. When the Colonists settled in America, they brought their English version of the Roman garden to the New England states. The formality and scale of the Roman style is seen along with many of the plants, which could survive in the English environment. The settlers, however, found new plants in America, which added to the Colonial plant palette.

The Georgian style's scale is grand with vertical forms and large, majestic trees. Many buildings are fronted with expansive, formal, rectangular lawns framed with a single row of hedge and an accent row of annual flowers. Plants commonly seen in the Georgian style are Cedrus deodora, Ulmus americana, Myrtus communis, and Parthenocissus tricuspidata.

A second style that was introduced to America during the Georgian Era is the "English Garden," the most formal of landscape designs. The English had borrowed forms and elements of the Roman style, but with a zeal for regular pruning. No English garden is "low maintenance." In England, there is plenty of water from normal rainfall to support plant life, but the cold winters require that shrubs be tough evergreens or perennials to survive.

Tightly manicured hedges with contrasting layers of green like Boxwood and Ligustrum are most common. Trees are grandiose and turf areas are expansive. Layout of hedged plant material is symmetrical, using rows of shrubs pruned into squares and rectangles. Topiaries are frequently seen in this style. Often, the hedged shrubs become borders for flower beds of roses or other flowering perennials.

Plant Palette

Trees

Abies grandis	Grand Fir
Acer rubrum	Red Maple
Acer saccharum	Sugar Maple
Betula nigra	Black Birch
Catalpa sp.	Indian Bean
Cedrus deodora	Deodora Cedar
Cedrus atlantica 'Glauca'	Blue Atlas Cedar
Celtis occidentalis	Hackberry
Cercis canadensis	Redbud
Cratageus sp.	Hawthorn
Fagus sp.	Beech
Fraxinus sp.	Ash Tree
Ginkgo biloba	Ginkgo
Juglans nigra	Black Walnut
Koelreuteria paniculata	Golden Rain Tree
Magnolia sp.	Magnolia
Liquidambar styraciflua	American Sweet Gum
Picea sp.	Spruce
Pinus pinea	Italian Stone Pine
Platanus acerfolia	London Plane Tree
Populus sp.	Poplar
Prunus caroliniana	Carolina Laurel Cherry
Prunus c. 'Atropurpurea'	Purple-leaf Plum
Prunus sp.	Edible Cherry
Pseudotsuga menziesii	Douglas Fir
Quercus sp.	Oak
Salix babylonica	Weeping Willow
Sorbus sp.	Mountain Ash
Ulmus americana	American Elm
Thuja occidentalis	Arborvitae
Tilia sp.	Linden
Tsuga sp.	Hemlock

Shrubs

Arctostaphylus sp.	Manzanita
Berberis thunbergii	Barberry
Betula alba	White Birch
Buddleja sp.	Butterfly Bush
Buxus microphylla	Japanese Boxwood
Camellia japonica	Camellia
Chaenomeles praecox	Quince
Cornus florida	Dogwood
Cotoneaster sp.	Cotoneaster
Drimys winteri	Winter's Bark
Eleagnus pungens	Silverberry
Euonymus sp.	ncn
Fuchsia hybrida	Fuchsia
Hydrangea sp.	Hydrangea
Ilex sp.	Holly
Juniperus sp.	Juniper
Leptospermum sp.	Tea Tree
Ligustrum japonicum	Japanese Privet
Myrtus communis	Common Myrtle
Osmanthus fragrans	Sweet Olive
Philadelphus sp.	Mock Orange
Phormium tenax	New Zealand Flax
Pittosporum sp.	Pittosporum
Rhododendron sp.	Azalea
Ribes sp.	Evergreen Currant
Rosa sp.	Rose
Sambucus sp.	Elderberry

Sorbus sp.	Mountain Ash	Lonicera sp.	Honeysuckle
Spiraea sp.	Spiraea	Parthenocissus tricuspidata	Boston Ivy
Syringa vulgaris	Common Lilac	Wisteria sinensis	Chinese Wisteria
Taxus baccata	English Yew		
Viburnum sp.	Viburnum	***Groundcovers***	
		Iris sp.	Iris
Vines			
Clematis sp.	Bower Vine		

Georgian Planting Design Concept

Georgian Planting Design

Concept
Formal, symmetrical, mostly manicured, with colorful flower beds, edible fruit, and use of native eastern United States plant material.

Trees
Large background evergreen mass: Picea sp. (Spruce) or Pseudotsuga menziesii (Douglas Fir)
Columnar midground: Populus sp. (Poplar) or Tilia sp. (Linden)
Picturesque foreground: Prunus sp. (Flowering Cherry)
Small foreground accent: Rosa sp. (Tree Rose)

Shrubs
Background hedge: Ligustrum japonicum (Japanese Privet)
Midground hedge: Ilex sp. (Holly)
Foreground hedge: Myrtus communis (Common Myrtle)
Pot accent: Iris sp. (Bearded Iris)

Vines and Groundcover
Climbing vine: Clematis sp.(Bower Vine)
Clumping foreground: Azalea indica (Southern Azalea)

Georgian planting design can be natural, like the natural landscape at Monticello with native hillside plantings beyond or semi-formal, like the downtown streetscape in Colonial Williamsburg, Virginia, or a formal English garden with green hedges and conifers. *(continued on following page)*

OPEN
GALLERY

English Garden Planting Design Concept

English Garden Planting Design

Concept
Very formal, symmetrical, and manicured contrasting greens, with mostly native trees, but virtually all ornamental shrubs.

Trees
Large background mass: Abies grandis (Grand Fir) and Juglans nigra (Black Walnut)
Columnar midground: Liquidambar styraciflua (American Sweet Gum) or Ginkgo biloba (Ginkgo)
Background column: Taxus baccata (English Yew)
Small foreground topiary: Juniperus scopularus (Columnar Juniper)

Shrubs
Background hedge: Ligustrum japonicum (Japanese Privet)
Midground hedge: Buxus japonica (Japanese Boxwood)
Foreground hedge: Euonymous sp. (ncn)
Pot accent: Phormium tenax (New Zealand Flax)
Clumping foreground: Azalea indica (Southern Azalea)

Chapter Five

VICTORIAN

Victorian • Stick • Queen Anne • Richardsonian • Romanesque • East Lake • Shingle • Exotic Eclectic • Folk Victorian

HISTORY

Contrary to popular thought, the term "Victorian" actually represents a period of architecture which occurred from about the middle to the end of the 1800s, during the reign of Queen Victoria of England (1837 to 1901). During this time, several innovations made it possible to create "Picturesque" architecture with many decorative elements. The development of the railroads made balloon framing and mass production of prefabricated construction products possible. Tools, hardware, paint, ornamental wood and ironwork, doors, windows, and building materials could be shipped across the United States.

In general, the technological breakthroughs of the late nineteenth century produced designs that were very asymmetrical with extensive ornamentation. The primary Victorian design styles generated are Stick, Queen Anne, Shingle, Richardsonian, and Second Empire. As time progressed, the styles of the Victorian era experienced both divergence and overlaps with each other. Many structures had predominant features from one style and additional elements from at least one other style.

Two pioneers of the Victorian Period were Architect Alexander Jackson Davis and Landscape Architect Andrew Jackson Downing. The two worked together to develop designs that brought a human scale by using unique ornamentation. Downing's writings were the first attempt by a landscape architect to apply fundamentals of landscape design to complement architecture. Had he not died at an early age, he likely would have been awarded the projects that made Fredrick Law Olmsted famous and the Father of Landscape Architecture.

A restored Stick home with patterning, exposed posts, beams, rafters, and railings from Heritage Park in San Diego, California.

THE STICK

Architectural Design

The first style that emerged during the American Victorian Period was the "Stick," a word created by Yale Professor Vincent J. Scully Jr. The theory of the Stick was to introduce pattern and texture into the blank walls with the use of applied stick work. The style took plain and monotonous walls and turned them into architectural canvases. One of the premier architects of the Victorian Period was Richard Morris Hunt. His design of the "Griswold House" in Newport, Rhode Island, was an introduction of the Stick style.

The Stick typically has a steep gable roof with cross gables and extended eaves with projecting brackets, rafter tails, diagonal or curving knee braces, and/or decorative trusses. The foundations were brick, holding walls with patterns of wood boards with horizontal, vertical, and diagonal members over a façade of clapboard or shingles. The patterns looked similar to half-timbering.

Distinctive Features

- Patterned Stickwork over clapboard walls
- Decorative brackets, rafters, trusses
- Simple doors and windows

An example of a Stick style home with wood-board and trim patterning for wall surfaces from Historic Downtown San Luis Obispo, California.

Site Design

Feature Integration

The Stick has complex geometrics with horizontal, vertical, diagonal, and curved patterns throughout. Providing an expanse of shingle or clapboard wood siding creates a canvas for ornamentation. False half-timbering and stickwork can be repeated in site design or created from scratch with 1x4 and 1x6 lumber construction.

Britt Scripps Inn in San Diego, California, is a fully restored Stick style mansion that also has some Queen Anne style features. The three-story turret and chimneystack reach above the downtown skyline. The garden and landscape reflect the architecture well.

Stick Forms

Materials and Finishes

As with all Victorian design, the basic plan view layout for the Stick is informal. To match the style of the Stick, landscape structures should be wood-framed with veneer materials consisting of primarily wood siding and milled lumber trim and faux half-timbering in vertical, horizontal, diagonal, and curved patterns. The Stick color palette is vast. Where building adjacent to the architecture, wood site elements need to duplicate the colors of that architecture. If creating a stand-alone structure, the Stick allows the designer to create any combination of colors with no wrong answer. Combinations are usually three or four primary colors, but can be as many as ten. The goal is for the finish to join the decorative trim patterns in giving the design character.

Brick and stone should be used sparingly. Where they are used, it should be common used brick with no decorative patterning or simple river rock rubble. Remember, the wood is the ornamentation for this style. Steel is normally not used and not recommend for remaining true to this style.

Color Palette

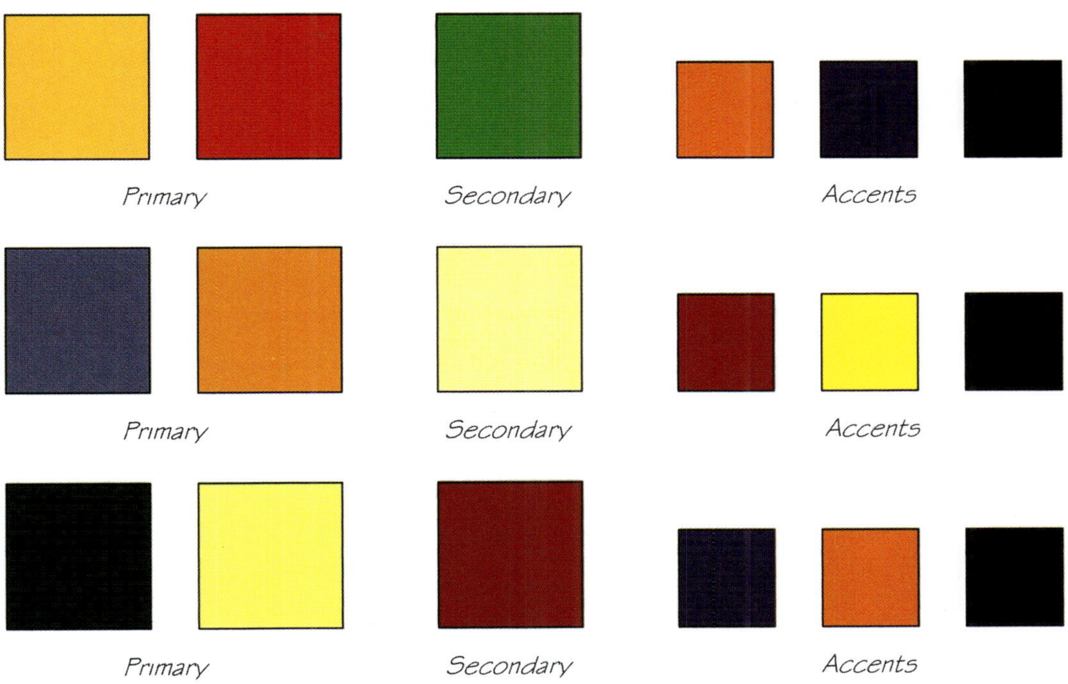

The Victorian style has a full spectrum of colors. These southern California Stick homes show some of the variety of color palettes.

Paving Design Concepts

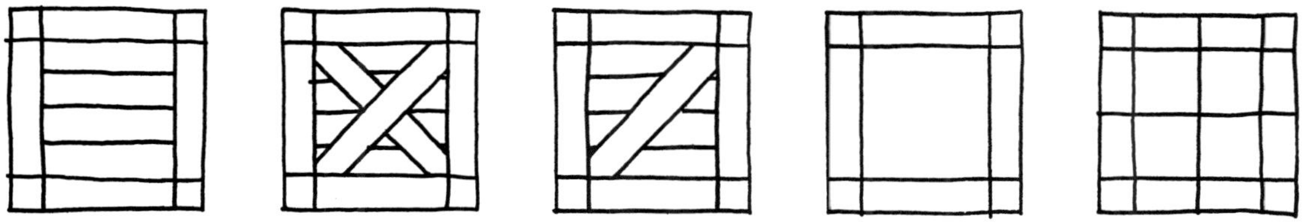

Paving

The best option for Stick paving would be wood decking. However, in most cases, this would be impractical to design. So to keep the focus on wood patterning, hardscape paving should be simple with plain natural color concrete, but can have patterned scoring. Steps and stepping pads should be plain natural color concrete. Steps can have a flush riser or be cantilever.

Fence Design Concepts

Walls and Fences

The Stick's use of wood provides an unlimited number of options for fencing. Design can start with horizontal or vertical siding or a combination of both. Every end of siding is framed by milled 1x4 or 1x6 trim. The remaining canvas can be divided with more trim and then filled with false half-timbering of vertical, horizontal, diagonal, and curved decorative patterns.

Trellises

Without the siding beneath, false half-timbering patterns can be repeated in Stick trellises. The patterns allow many options for creativity and vine growth.

Shade Covers

Use of wood makes the Stick one of the best styles for designing trellises, arbors, and gazebos. Each of these structures can accommodate the traditional Stick decorative patterning between post and rail design. They need to be painted with the primary color palette common to the Stick.

Shade Cover Design Concepts

Seating

Tables and benches for the Stick are wood construction with milled, undressed lumber for arms and legs. Backrests are false half-timbering. Benches are finished in the Stick primary colors, maintaining the toy store-like quality.

QUEEN ANNE

Architectural Design

During the Arts and Crafts movement, the British saw the rise of the Queen Anne style. Henry Hobson Richardson was the first to design a building in America using this style with "Sherman House" in Newport, Rhode Island. The Queen Anne was fully introduced to America at the Philadelphia Centennial Exposition of 1876. Americans added ornate scrollwork and extensive detailing, not typical in England. In America, most examples are wood, while in England, most are brick masonry.

Probably the most recognized and extravagant Queen Anne style residence is Carson House in Eureka, California, with it's asymmetrical design, steep roofs, and exaggerated spindlework. *Courtesy of the Eureka Historical Society.*

These two Queen Anne residences, among others, at Heritage Park in San Diego, California, have been restored to their original condition.

The Queen Anne is the style most visualized as "Victorian." It is identified by its full-width single-story porch and steep, irregular roof (often with a turret), shingled façade, and decorative surface patterning. Like the Stick, the Queen Anne uses wall surfaces for decoration with shingle patterns, knee braces, and brackets. The Queen Anne goes further than the Stick in wall ornamentation. Where the Stick uses false half-timbering patterns to create interesting designs, the Queen Anne uses shapes, patterning, and color variation of shingles or siding.

Unlike the Stick, the Queen Anne has a dominant hipped roof with several cross gables. It is more ornamented with jig-sawn scrollwork on eaves and overhangs. It also has lacy, lathed spindle work for posts and balustrades. In addition to the full-length verandah, most of the Queen Anne designs include a gazebo and a tower element. Windows are normally one over one or twelve over one. There is usually an ornate brick chimney with masonry molding. "Carson House," built in 1884, in Eureka, California, is one of the most defining examples.

The sub-style "East Lake" was the most elaborate of the Queen Anne, incorporating all these elements to their extreme.

Hutchins House in Pasadena, California, was relocated from it's original site and restored in the mid-1900s. The current owners are committed to retaining the Queen Anne mansion's historic value.

The Apple Farm in San Luis Obispo, California, was designed to reflect the historic value of its hometown. The verandah is a common Queen Anne feature.

Stevens House in Historic Downtown Tustin, California, has one of the most distinguishable and unique turrets. The turrets common to the Queen Anne style provide the landscape designer with an excellent source for gazebo design inspiration.

This style can be seen in several of the works produced by Thomas Kinkade, Painter of Light. Kinkade's tours of the towns, which sprung up in the late 1800s along the northern coast of California, provided inspiration with their abundance of Queen Anne buildings.

Distinctive Features

- Irregular Structure with trim framed edges and corners
- Full-length verandah and round or octagonal tower
- Elaborate scrollwork and spindlework

Heritage Square in Los Angeles, California, contains several salvaged, relocated, and restored Queen Anne style homes. Note the ornate chimneystack on the home shown above.

SITE DESIGN

Feature Integration

The irregular shapes found in the Queen Anne allow many options for plan view design. Rectangular, circular, and octagonal forms contribute to the overall informal layout. Like the Stick, the primary features transferable from the Queen Anne are wood elements, but in the form of scrollwork and spindlework. Detail in the spindlework can be repeated in the landscape. Verandahs and tower elements on architecture provide examples easy to translate into the landscape. Where architecture has decorative fireplaces, the forms can be repeated in walls and outdoor fire features.

Various Queen Anne style residences built at the end of the nineteenth century in California soon after the completion of the Central Pacific Railroad. Once homes to the wealthy, these have now become historical landmarks, museums, and Inns. *(continued on following 3 pages)*

556

Queen Anne Forms

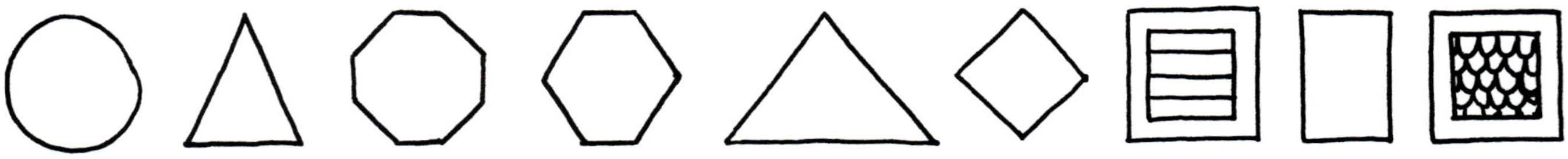

Materials and Finishes

The predominant material used in Queen Anne design is wood. The wood's required high-maintenance is why so many of the Victorian Era historical buildings have disappeared. Termites, dry rot, and frequent need for painting were the reason this style didn't last and has not seen a revival. I suppose if someone was interested in fabricating Queen Anne building materials using a low-maintenance product, there could be a revival of this style. Especially since the design is vertical, fitting with modern goals of maximizing building to land ratio.

Wood is for structural construction and also for facades. On the building walls, the canvas created by the Queen Anne's trim framing is filled with either wood siding or shingles. While the Stick style is designed with simple, squared shingles, the Queen Anne has complex decorative shingles, with filleted (dog-ear) or rounded edge overlapping. Shingles are often arranged in decorative patterns, either by shape or by color.

Steel and concrete are not used in this style. Though the Queen Anne style is limited to mostly wood design, if hardscape materials are used sparingly and designed to be decorative and even busy, they can still remain consistent with the style. Where brick is used, it should be common red brick with variations in vertical relief and in horizontal layering.

Another difference between the Stick and the Queen Anne is the color palette used to paint the wood surfaces. Normally, the color palette is limited to only two or three colors. The main color (covering the wood siding or shingles) is typically a pastel-like yellow chiffon, pink, or baby blue. The secondary color is white, which covers all the wood trim, spindlework, and scrolling. Often a third bright accent color is added.

Color Palette

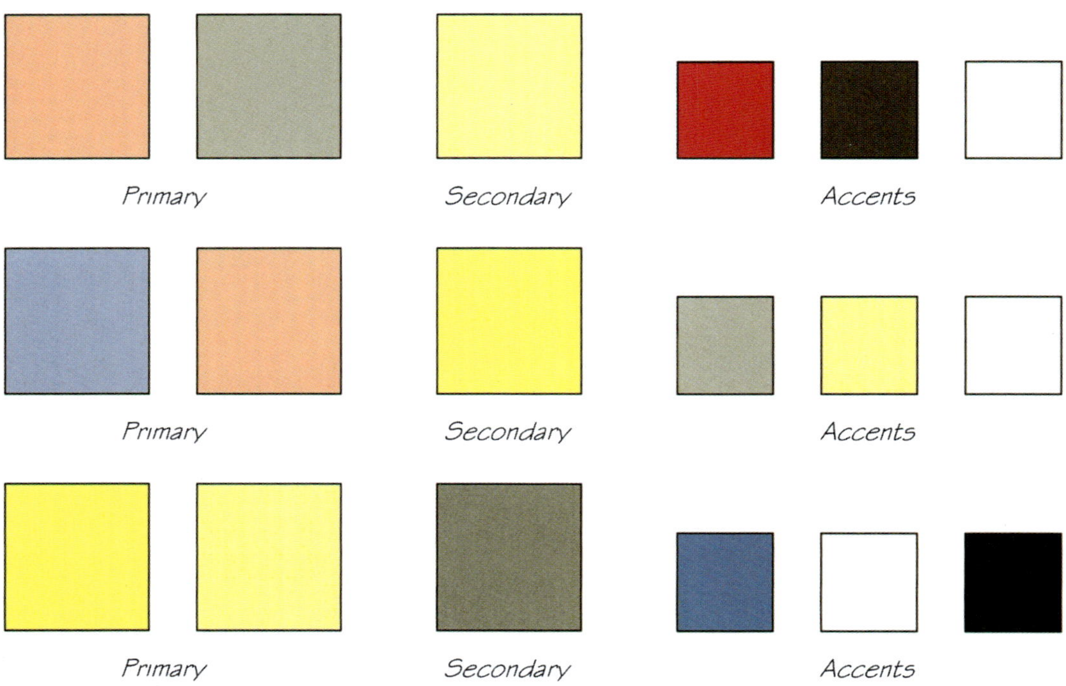

Paving Design Concepts

Paving

The decorative shingle patterning of the Queen Anne style can be reflected into paving with the use of brick or concrete paving stones. For the traditional, common red brick is used with banding and decorative field patterns like herringbone or basket weave. A compatible design using modern materials would be a natural concrete band frame with paving stones inside for entries and nodes. For walkways, exposed aggregate concrete remains consistent with the Queen Anne ornamentation. Where steps are required, bullnose brick or squared concrete band treads can be used.

Fence Design Concepts

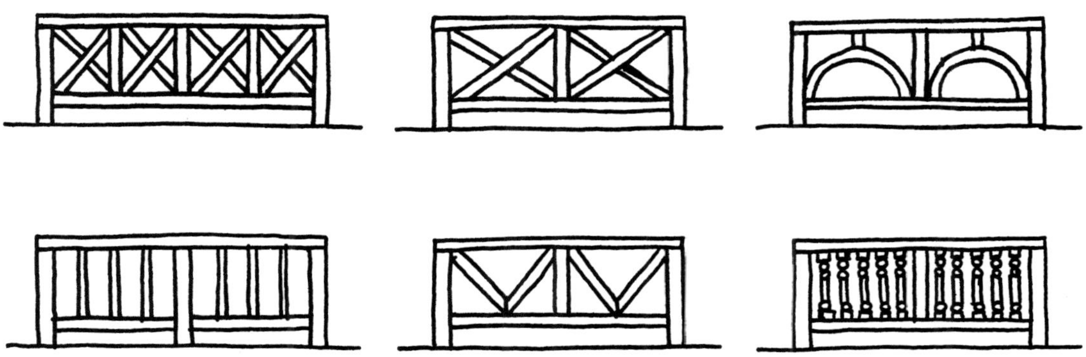

Walls and Fences

Since the Queen Anne style is primarily wood construction, masonry should be used sparingly. A wall constructed of all brick will likely appear as Georgian or Prairie. A better effect would be to use decorative brick pilasters with wood fencing in between. Solid wood fencing can integrate wood siding or shingle patterns between posts and rails. Open fencing should be wood picket with dog-ear or rounded end-cuts and other decorative cuts. The extreme would be to incorporate the lacy scrolling and spindlework from the Queen Anne verandah.

Trellises

Trellises for the Queen Anne are wood construction using the verandah scrolling and spindlework. A good example would be lattice between spindled posts with a decorative scrollwork top.

Shade Covers

The most common design for gazebos is the Queen Anne. Most wooden gazebo manufacturers like Amish Country Gazebos create designs reminiscent of the gazebos and turrets seen on Queen Anne style buildings. When these gazebos are built in the modern day, we normally see the entire structure finished in white paint. A more realistic representation of Queen Anne style would be to have latticework finished in a chiffon color with posts and rails in white. Spindled posts can have accents of a bright color. Gazebos are either round or octagonal.

Shade Cover Design Concepts

Seating

Tables and benches for the Queen Anne style are wood construction integrating spindlework for arms and legs. Backrests are an opportunity for elaborate laciness with lattice and scrollwork.

The intricacy of spindlework on this historical mansion in Redlands, California, shows the skill and craftsmanship required to build the Queen Anne style.

THE SHINGLE

Architectural Design

The "Shingle" has the same overall building form as the Queen Anne, but with no ornamentation, just complete coverage of natural wood shingles on all walls. No decorative doors, windows, spindlework, or scrollwork. Where corners and roof intersections for dormers and towers occur, shingles make the transition with soft curves instead of hard edges. Louvered shutters usually complement the simple windows. The natural wood is normally accompanied by a chimney made of indigenous stone. The impression this style gives is that the owner is not very interested in entertaining. Whether intended or not, for the most part, it appears dark and uninviting.

Distinctive Features

- Irregular Structure, with rounded edges and corners
- Complete shingle coverage
- No ornamentation
- A dark, secluded appearance

Site Design

Feature Integration

The simple forms used in the Shingle actually come from the landscape, so they are easily integrated. The rounded eyebrow dormers and corners resemble natural, rolling hills. The landscape must appear natural and non-engineered, very informal. As with most other Victorian structures, wood construction is used for most site design elements. The stone chimney can be reflected in hardscape elements.

Shingle Forms

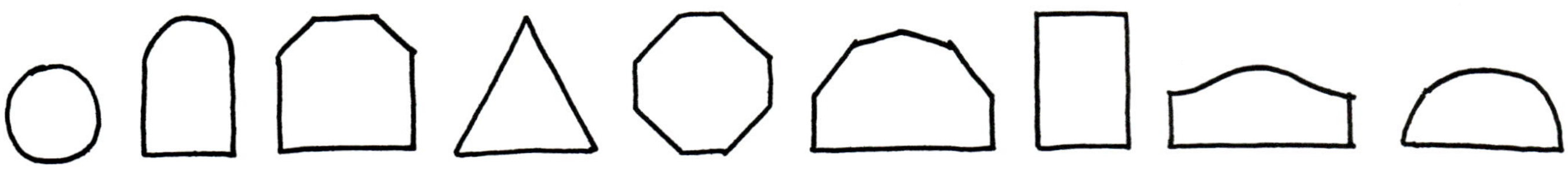

This restored residence from Heritage Square in Los Angeles shows the precursor to the Shingle style. Note that although wood siding was used, the dormer and building forms common to the Shingle were emerging.

Materials and Finishes

The overall look of the Shingle is very minimalist and natural, using unfinished split cedar shingles to cover every surface of a structure. The Shingle is the harbinger to the use of natural form and materials like in the Craftsman and Prairie styles. The structure is all wood except for the use of indigenous stone. No wood is painted, no concrete is colored, and no stone is cut.

Color Palette

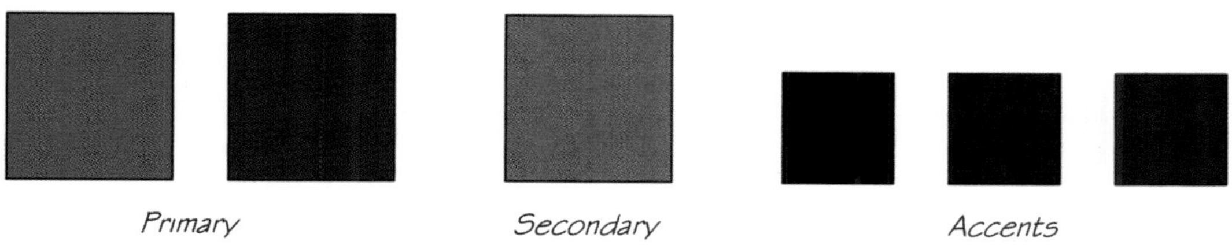

Paving Design Concepts

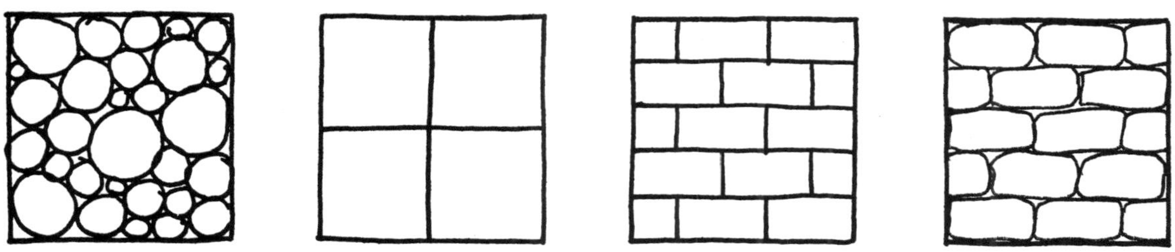

Paving

Paving for the Shingle must maintain a minimalist, natural appearance, so decks and walks should integrate quarry (un-cut) stone. Walkways can be plain, natural color concrete or exposed aggregate paving. Field areas can be natural stone paving. Wood decks should be constructed using simple wood planking, with no decoration.

Steps should be natural stone or natural concrete with either a flush riser or a simple square cantilever: plain, natural color concrete with radiused riser, no cantilever. Stepping pads should be large, natural stone.

Walls and Fences

The Shingle's design really only lends itself to solid wood fence construction. Existing Shingle fences are almost always solid with overlapping rows of natural shingles. There is not opportunity for ornamentation. The other possibility is to use natural dry-stacked stone for walls and planters.

Trellises

Given the nature of the Shingle design, there is little inspiration to be had and few forms which may be incorporated into the trellis design. If trellises are desired, the design should be very simple wood construction.

Shade Cover Design Concepts

Shade Covers

Probably the best opportunity to integrate the Shingle into the landscape is through shade cover design. Rather than using posts, Shingle shade cover design should have wood-frame walls with openings for windows. The walls and the roof must be completely covered with shingles.

Richardsonian

Architectural Design

Henry Hobson Richardson created a style that took its primary form and elements from the Queen Anne and added Medieval components and materials. Of all the styles from the Victorian Era, this was the most unique. His later termed "Richardsonian" style used large block masonry stonework instead of wood for walls. He used multiple types and colors of cut stone to create round features like archways, towers, and porch columns. Windows were almost always double hung, one over one. The overall look is a stronger, more solid structure, but still with delicate touches.

Distinctive Features

- Irregular Structure
- Large block stonework facade
- Medieval towers or columned archways

The San Luis Obispo County Historical Museum resides within this restored Richardsonian style residence.

The Richardsonian style's large scale form and materials are ideal for large public buildings as shown by the Orange County Courthouse in Santa Ana, California.

SITE DESIGN

Feature Integration

The Richardsonian is probably the easiest Victorian Era style to integrate into the landscape because of its use of forms and materials. Many Richardsonian buildings have cut stone archways, turrets, and wall designs that can be repeated for site design. Site layout is informal, but with massive geometric forms, not natural or ornate. A steep conical turret can be found on almost every design.

Though the Richardsonian style best fits large buildings, the use of this style for residential structures creates a sense of implied security, similar to the Gothic style.

Richardsonian Forms

Materials and Finishes

The Richardsonian is the one Victorian Era style with the materials that will prevail over time. The cut stone blocks are usually gray or earth tones. To integrate this style of design into the modern landscape, walls can be constructed with CMU masonry and faced with larger veneer units.

The color palette for the Richardsonian is subdued. It is neither primary colors with a toy store quality, nor a chiffon selection of soft feminine colors, nor a natural unfinished color selection. It is a more masculine palette of colors, almost like a gentleman's three-piece gray suit with a single-color necktie accent for doors or special roof elements.

Color Palette

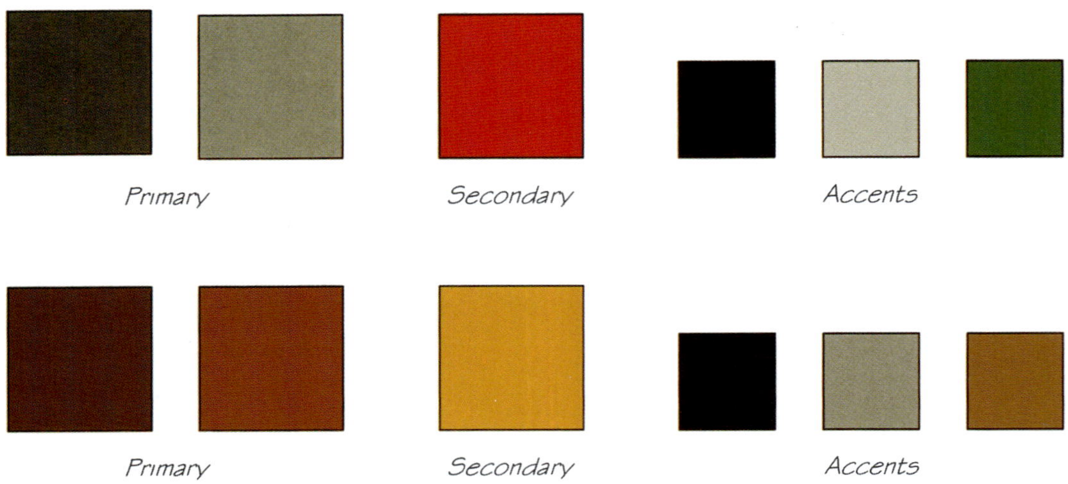

Paving Design Concepts

Paving

A Richardsonian style paving design uses large paving units. Massive concrete pavers or cut stones with no grout joints are consistent with the style. Where long distances of walkway are needed, plain natural color concrete with straight scorelines can be used. If banding is used, it should be straight cut-stone bands.

The massive block units can be used for steps with an angled, not radiused cantilever tread. Stepping pads should be fields of large cut-stone or informally placed, rectangular-shaped, plain natural color concrete.

Walls

The Richardsonian can easily be translated into wall design with its use of large cut-stone, block masonry. There are opportunities for interesting pilaster designs using turret and castellations. Even with standard square pilasters, the use of large block and blocky mass can create a look consistent with the style.

Fence Design Concepts

Fences

To be consistent with the Richardsonian style, fencing does not have to be wood, but can be wrought iron. Whatever the material, the design should be simple. Gothic fencing examples can be used.

Trellises

The best design for Richardsonian trellises would be black wrought iron designed with a non-ornate Gothic style influence. Elements like spears and finials need to remain simple.

Shade Cover Design Concepts

Shade Covers

Using the inspiration from Richardsonian turrets and castellations, gazebos can be designed for this style. The use of cut stone results in a round plan view form. Turret-like features are tapered with a wide base and narrowing with height. Cut-stone archways can be incorporated for openings.

Depending on the sub-style, Victorian paving can have a broad range, but should be an informal layout of paving stones or cobbles.

Victorian paving can include decorative layout of cobbles. This example from Casita Verde Los Angeles, California, also shows the use of native stonework with decorative caps.

These walls from Kimberly-Crest House in Redlands, California, show a more formal flavor, but with some Victorian ornamentation.

This wall and fence combination at Britt Scripps Inn shows both Richardsonian and Queen Anne influences.

Victorian trellis structures are informal, but decorative.

These gazebos provide just three of the many designs that can evolve from the Queen Anne style.

This Queen Anne style turret rises above the Sycamore trees in Heritage Square, Los Angeles; this turret provides a possible gazebo inspiration.

This turret is good inspiration for a Shingle or Richardsonian shade cover.

Victorian water features can range from informal to semi-formal. *(continued on following page)*

Built during the Victoria Era, Kimberly-Crest House in Redlands, California, was inspired to be a French Chateau, but has semi-Classical design elements like this sun dial located adjacent to a walled lily pond.

An informal Victoria garden with ornamental steel furnishings. *Courtesy of the Queen Victorian Inn.*

PLANTING DESIGN

In America, the Victorian style emerged in the East, but gained tremendous popularity in the West where the plant palette increased with flowering shrubs and vines able to withstand the seasons. When discussing a planting design that is Victorian, traditionally it is associated with the Stick and Queen Anne styles. For a Shingle style planting design, the Craftsman plant palette can be combined with the Victorian. For the Richardsonian, a Gothic style palette can be combined with the Victorian.

The traditional Victorian style planting design (what is used for the Stick and the Queen Anne) is a paradox of design. Occurring between the Georgian Era and the Craftsman Era, it combines formal design with the informal. It typically has borders of formal hedges with a contrasting asymmetrical layout of trees and flowering shrubs and vines.

The use of formal hedges creates planting areas for the shrubs and perennials one would typically see in the French Country garden. The Victorian style's intricately detailed architecture is reflected in the landscape with the use of fine textured flowers and foliage. It has lacy fine textures like the elegance and femininity of a queen. Dark shrub hedges contrast with colorful bouquets of flowers. The Victorian style spares no expense in detail and quality.

In the West, technology and society at the end of the nineteenth century brought influences to the plant palette. Most specifically, the citrus orchards in California influenced property owners to use orange, lemon, and avocado trees in planting designs. The Victorian style design's use of verandas introduced the use of flowering vines on the building structure. Most Victorian planting designs mimic the design of the building by having a single vertical element as the primary focal point. Similar to having a turret, many Victorian designs have a single, large tree. Phoenix canariensis and Cedrus deodora were the most popular trees. Sometimes pines or oaks were used.

Some semi-formal Victoria planting designs with asymmetrical hedge rows and colorful flowers. *Courtesy of the Inn at 22 Jackson Street and the Queen Victorian Inn.* *(continued on following two pages)*

JACKSON

Plant Palette

Trees

Acer saccharinum	Silver Maple
Aesculus hippocastanum	Horse Chestnut
Bauhinia purpurea	Orchid Tree
Betula pendula	White Birch
Cedrus deodora	Deodora Cedar
Cedrus atlantica 'Glauca'	Blue Atlas Cedar
Citrus sp.	Orange, Lemon
Cupressus sempervirens	Italian Cypress
Gleditsia triacanthos	Honey Locust
Laburnum sp.	Golden Chain Tree
Lagerstroemia indica	Crape Myrtle
Liriodendron tulipfera	Tulip Tree
Liquidambar styraciflua	American Sweet Gum
Magnolia soulangeana	Saucer Magnolia
Magnolia grandiflora	Southern Magnolia
Malus sp.	Crab Apple
Persea americana	Avocado
Phoenix canariensis	Canary Island Palm
Pinus sp.	Pine
Pittosporum undulatum	Victorian Box
Prunus caroliniana	Carolina Laurel Cherry
Prunus c. 'Atropurpurea'	Purple-leaf Plum
Prunus sp.	Edible Cherry
Pyrus calleryana	Ornamental Pear
Robinia pseudoacacia	Black Locust
Quercus sp.	Oak
Ulmus americana	American Elm

Shrubs

Abelia grandiflora	Glossy Abelia
Azalea indica	Southern Azalea
Buddleja davidii	Butterfly Bush
Buxus microphylla japonica	Japanese Boxwood
Calluna vulgaris	Scotch Heather
Camellia japonica	Camellia
Catalpa sp.	Indian Bean
Chamelacium uncinatum	Waxflower
Cuphea hyssopifolia	Mexican Heather
Diosma pulchrum	Pink Breath of Heaven
Erica sp.	Heather
Escallonia sp.	Pink Princess
Euryops sp.	Yellow Bush Daisy
Felicia amelloides	Blue Marguerite
Fuschia hybrida	Fuschia
Hydrangea sp.	Hydrangea
Juniperus sp.	Juniper
Lathyrus sp.	Sweet Pea
Lavandula sp.	Lavender
Ligustrum japonica	Japanese Privet
Leptospermum sp.	Tea Tree
Osmanthus fragrans	Sweet Olive
Myrsine africana	African Boxwood
Myrtus communis	Common Myrtle
Philapelphus sp.	Mock Orange
Rhaphiolepis indica	Indian Hawthorn
Rosa sp.	Rose
Rosmarinus officinalis	Rosemary
Spiraea sp.	Spiraea
Syringa vulgaris	Common Lilac
Thymus vulgaria	Thyme
Viburnum odoratissimum	Sweet Viburnum

Vines and Espaliers

Beaumontia grandiflora	Easter Lily Vine
Bignonia violacea	Purple Trumpet Vine
Bougainvillea sp.	Bougainvillea
Campsis sp.	Trumpet Creeper
Clematis sp.	Bower Vine
Gelsimium sempervirens	Carolina Jasmine
Grewia occidentalis	Lavender Starflower
Ipomoea sp.	Morning Glory
Lonicera japonica	Giant Honeysuckle
Mandevilla sp.	Mandevilla
Jasminum polyanthum	Pink Jasmine
Wisteria sinensis	Chinese Wisteria

Groundcover

Bergenia crassifolia	Bergenia
Cosmos sp.	Cosmos
Digitalis sp.	Foxglove
Juniperus sp.	Juniper
Hedera helix	English Ivy
Lantana montevidensis	Trailing Lantana
Verbena peruviana	Verbena
Vinca minor	Common Periwinkle

A true Victorian garden has an informal layout, featuring a single vertical specimen tree like a Cedar or a Date Palm. This concept is similar to having a single turret for buildings. Plants common to Victorian garden design were Citrus trees, vines on verandas, and hedges for borders.

Planting Design Concept

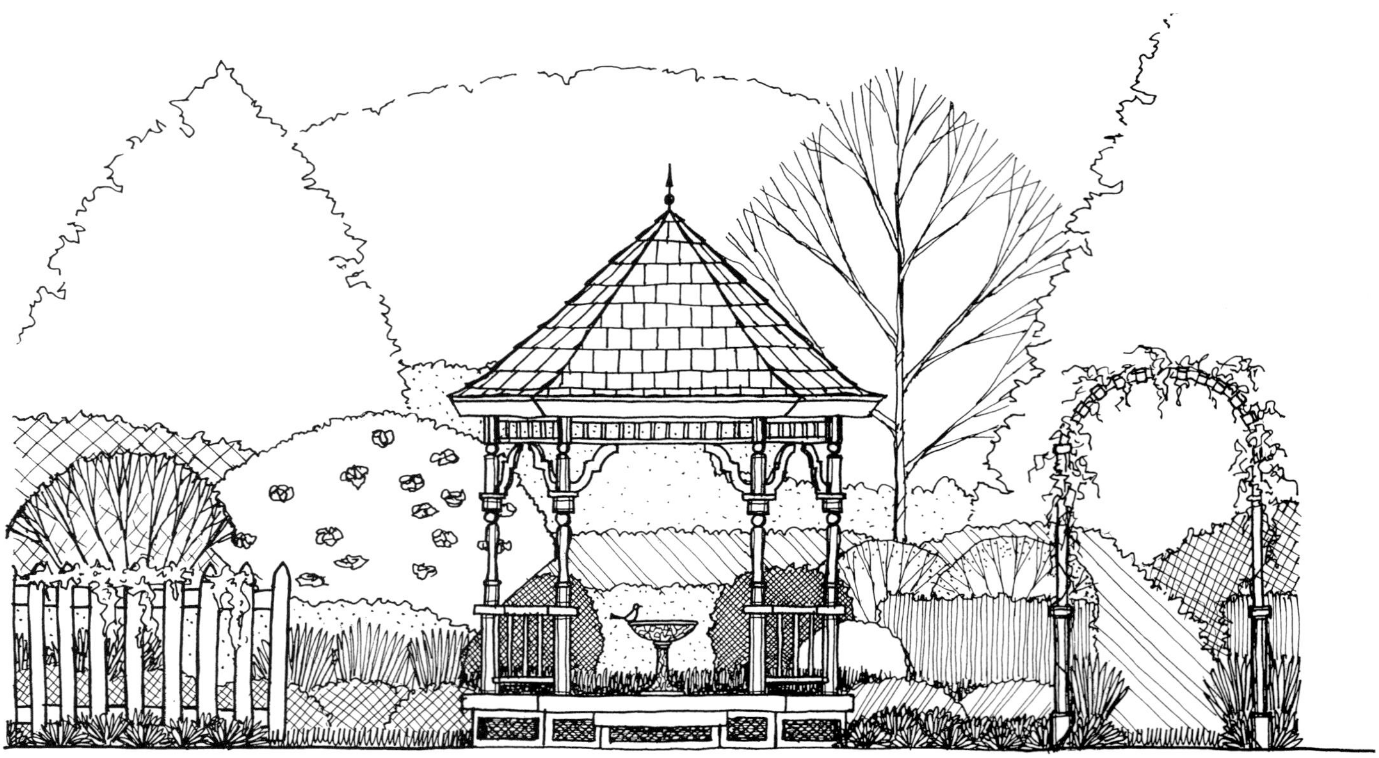

Victorian Planting Design

Concept
Informal, contrasting form, multiple flower color, and fine texture emphasis. Many flowering and edible fruit plants.

Trees
Large background mass: Ulmus americana (American Elm)
Vertical midground conifer: Pinus sp. (Pine)
Vertical midground deciduous: Acer saccharinum (Silver Maple)
Picturesque midground vertical specimen: Cedrus atlantica 'Glauca' (Blue Atlas Cedar)
Foreground flowering accent: Magnolia soulangeana (Saucer Magnolia)
Foreground form accent: Prunus c. 'Atropurpurea' (Purple-leaf Plum)

Shrubs
Background mass: Viburnum odoratissimum (Sweet Viburnum)
Background mass: Escallonia sp. (Pink Princess)
Background flowering mass: Buddleja davidii (Butterfly Bush)
Midground hedge: Buxus japonica microphylla (Japanese Boxwood)
Midground flowering mass: Leptospermum sp. (Tea Tree)
Midground flowering accent: Felicia amelloides (Blue Marguerite)
Foreground hedge: Myrtus communis (Common Myrtle)
Foreground medium accent: Hydrangea sp. (Hydrangea)
Foreground flowering accent: Azalea indica (Southern Azalea)
Foreground flowering accent: Lavandula sp. (Lavender)

Vines
Twining fence vine: Mandevilla splendens (Evergreen Mandevilla)
Flowering arbor vine: Jasminum polyanthum (Pink Jasmine)

Groundcover
Foreground clumping: Bergenia crassifolia (Bergenia)
Foreground trailing: Hedera helix (Needlepoint Ivy)

An informal garden featuring an ornate Queen Anne style gazebo.

Chapter Six
ITALIAN

Italian • Italianate • Villa Italian Renaissance • Italian Renaissance Revival • Second Italian Renaissance Revival • Tuscan

HISTORY

The first appearance of Italian architecture in America was Cronkhill, designed by John Nash in 1802. The design was termed the "Italian Villa" and resembled buildings in northern Italy. Nash's (as was other architect's of the time) design was inspired by landscape paintings by French Romanticist Artists. The Italian Villa design flourished from 1845 to 1870. During this "Italian Renaissance," another style, the "Italianate," emerged and continued even beyond the time of the Villa. Though there were a number of variations in designs, these are the two primary, identifiable Italian sub-styles. At the end of this period, Andrew Jackson Downing published "Victorian Cottage Residences," an excellent resource for understanding the architectural style and design thought process of that era. Most of his examples were of Italian Villas and the Italianate style.

From 1890 to 1930, another "Italian Renaissance" occurred, which promoted an attempt to mimic the Italian Palazzo. This was the first "Mediterranean" style. One of the leading designs was "Villard House," built in New York in 1883.

The countryside of Castiglion in Fiorentino, Italy. Notice the low-pitched roofs and earth-tone building walls. *Courtesy of Megan Flanagan.*

The skyline surrounding Ponteveccio in Florence, Italy. Notice the multistory buildings, tower elements, and full arches. *Courtesy of Megan Flanagan.*

Italian Villa and Italianate

Architectural Design

The main differences between the Italian Villa and the Italianate are the former has a more complex (not simple) asymmetrical structure and normally has a tower element, often with a copula. The Villa also has a loggia or veranda, which is absent on the Italianate.

Both sub-styles have the distinctive Italian features: a multi-story building with a shallow-pitched hipped roof having a broad overhang and decorative bracketing. The Italianate is often called the "American Bracketed." Italian architecture has smooth walls, with tall, round-top arches in either 2 on 2 or 4 on 4 double-hung designs. Windows are often in pairs or triplets. In addition to crowned window arches, Italian designs have belt courses to define building level transitions and other crown moldings. Although the Italianate lacked a tower, it normally had a symmetrically placed copula or roof lantern.

The Gonzales County Courthouse in Texas is an example of Italian Villa architecture with an asymmetrical design, multiple stories, grouped arches, bracketed eaves, and a single tower element. *Courtesy of Bob Weston.*

The design of this mansion housing Plymouth Village in Redlands, California, allows one to easily identify it as Italian Villa by the broad, overhanging eaves and bracketing. Notice the amount of shade cast on the tower from the eaves.

Some of the building variations had smooth block construction, quoins, fully pedimented windows, elaborate cornices, balustraded balconies, and columned entries. The Tuscan and the Lombard are examples of sub-styles of the first Italian Renaissance.

Distinctive Features

- Multi-story structure
- Italian Villa – asymmetrical with loggia and tower and copula
- Italianate – symmetrical with copula or roof lantern only
- Low-pitched hipped roof with eave brackets
- Round-top arches with crown molding

Two examples of Italianate inspired architectural design: Christ Church in Los Angeles, California, and Pomona Unified School District Education Center in Pomona, California, showing symmetrical design, broad overhangs, shallow-pitched roofs, and large masonry units.

Italian Renaissance Revival

Architectural Design

Sometimes termed the "Second Italian Renaissance," taking place from 1890 to 1930, this revival introduced some new features to the Italian style. The style was to emulate the Italian Palazzo by using an arched palladian (a projecting, often classical columned) and portico or recessed loggia. The symmetrical structure had a hipped roof covered with Spanish red tile and the walls for the first floor were often limestone block with stucco on other wall surfaces, emphasizing the first floor.

St. Peter's Square at the Vatican in Rome, Italy, demonstrates the Classical influence on Italian architecture. This inspired inclusion of these elements in Italian Renaissance Revival architectural design.

To expand the interest of the arch, the second renaissance brought the arch section and the corner radiused rectangle. The arches were always present on the first floor in doors and windows. The second floor windows were de-emphasized by being smaller and/or rectangular.

Distinctive Features

- Symmetrical structure with design emphasis on first floor
- Hipped Spanish red-tile roof
- Arched and columned palladian

The Los Angeles skyline is replete with examples of Italian Renaissance Revival architecture.

SITE DESIGN

Feature Integration

To distinguish between the different period styles as they pertain to the landscape, when mentioning the Italian Villa and Italianate, they can be considered the "Traditional" Italian style. The late 1800s movement of the Italian Renaissance Revival is considered the "Revival" style.

The features that are common to Italian architecture and can be integrated into the landscape are geometric straight lines, groupings of round-top arches with crown molding, Classical or Tuscan columns, eave bracketing under a low-pitched, hipped barrel red-tile roof, and the use of symmetrical design layout (except for the asymmetrical Italian Villa).

The Italian Villa offers design possibilities for loggias and towers, while the Italianate provides examples for using copulas and roof lanterns. The Revival's contributions to design are the arched and columned palladian, large cut stone veneering, and the addition of decorative detailing.

The Masonic Temple in Pamona, California, is an unmistakable example of Italian Renaissance Revival architecture with masonry walls, bracketing, non-arched windows, and the added Classical columned portico entry.

Italian Forms

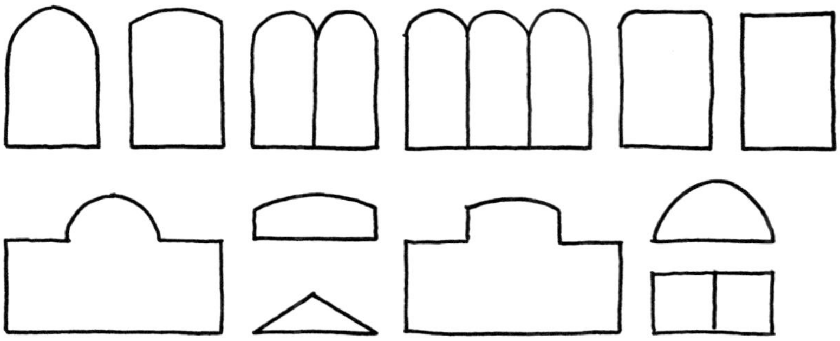

Materials and Finishes

The common material for the Italian style is white or off-white smooth plaster. Wood is used for framing and is also used as a decorative element. The bracketing is a repetition of special end-cuts that can be repeated in wood construction for site elements like fencing, trellises, shade covers, and site furnishings. Wood elements are finished in dark brown.

Natural color concrete is used for paving, decorative pre-cast moldings, and pre-cast concrete columns. The Revival introduced large cut stone blocks, which can be used for large-scale wall design. Where decorative stone is used, it should be cut or at least stacked angular stone in warm colors.

Where steel is included in an Italian design, it is typically moderately decorative wrought iron fencing with a glossy black finish. Sometimes dark brown is used. Specialty materials are red barrel tile roofing and red floor tile.

Recent design has yielded some intriguing variations of the Italian style. These buildings from The Village in Irvine, California, show the incorporation of various Italian features.

Color Palette

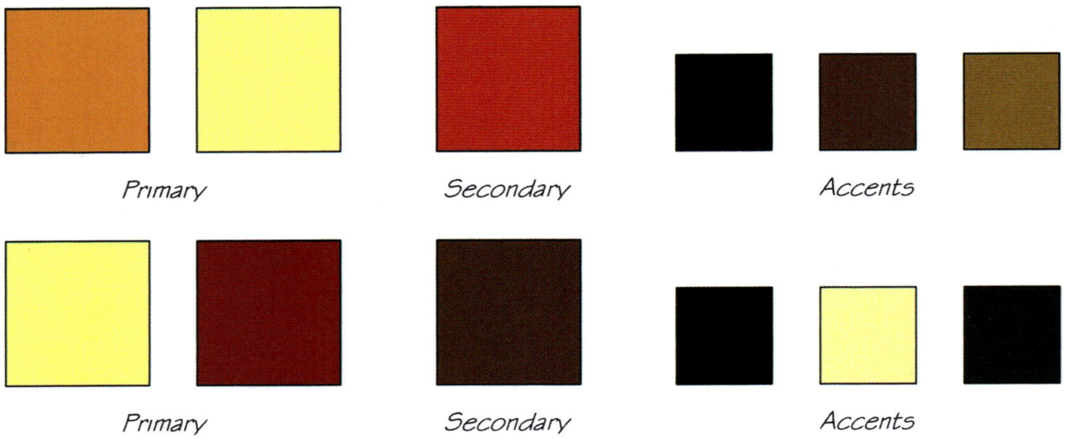

Paving Design Concepts

Paving

Layout of paving is straight and most likely symmetrical. The signature Italian arch can be repeated into landings and plaza areas. Where concrete is used, scoring is in symmetrical and equal squares. Modern paving for the Italian style is normally red tile with natural color concrete banding and borders. Traditional Italian paving is with warm colored cut clay or stone cobbles, which can also be translated into the landscape in the form of rectangular pre-cast concrete paving stones. Paving stones are to be placed in random ashlar patterns and can have straight, repetitious banding.

Steps are standard cantilever concrete or foam-formed cantilever concrete with tread nose molding. Where paving is decorative, step pads should be more than just natural concrete. The paving and concrete banding can be extended into stepping pad design. In natural gardens, natural random stepping-stones can replace the straight lines.

Some decorative formal paving designs from the resorts of Las Vegas, Nevada.

The design style for the St. Regis Resort and Spa in Laguna Niguel, California, is an extension of the Italian style into Mediterranean style with many features from both Italian and Classical design.

Cobble paving at The Village in Irvine.

Informal paving stepping pads in a garden at the St. Regis.

Wall Design Concepts

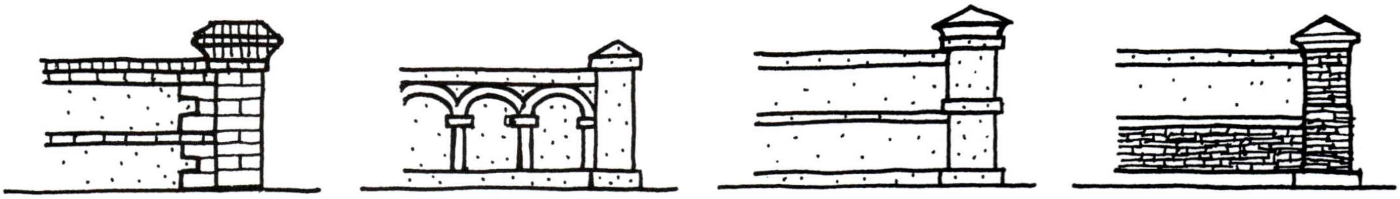

Walls

The primary Italian wall design material is smooth plaster. Walls typically have widened bases and caps with mitered edge moldings and are completely covered in white or off-white plaster. Sometimes decorative molded concrete caps can be used, but rarely is there additional adornment. Pilasters are squares to match the walls. Caps for walls are peaked and pilaster caps pyramided.

For added wall detail, architectural foam can be applied to create belt courses and Italian arch forms. Cut or angular stacked stone can be used in accent areas.

These formal Italian walls and pilasters at the St. Regis and the Bellagio Resort and Spa in Las Vegas have balustrading and pre-cast concrete molding. *(continued on following three pages)*

THE MIRAGE
LOVE

Fence Design Concepts

Fences

Italian style fencing can be dark brown-finished wood or black to dark brown-finished ornamental wrought iron. Solid fencing has vertical wood slat and posts that can have finials or decorative caps. Open wood fencing can be 1x lumber or square pickets extending above top rails. Where gates are designed, there is an opportunity to integrate the Italian arch form.

Wrought iron fencing can be designed with Classical detailing with spears for pickets and finials for post tops.

Trellises

Trellises can also be designed with wood or metal. A good Italian trellis integrates the arch form. As with other features, wood is finished in dark brown and metal in glossy black. Trellises can have added ornamentation with flanking posts and finials.

Italian design can include vine arbors. A possibility would be a series of archways with joining wire or lattice creating a corridor of grape vines.

Trellis and overhead structures with a traditional Italian appearance at The Village in Irvine.

Vine arbor designs from a residence, The Village and the Bellagio.

Shade Cover Design Concepts

Tuscan style shade covers.

Shade Covers

The features and materials indigenous to the Italian style create many opportunities for shade cover design. Solid roofs are low-pitched hipped with red barrel tile with overhanging eaves and supporting decorative-cut wood bracketing. An Italianate flavor would be to add a copula element at the roof peak. Open canopies are brown-finished rough-sawn lumber lattice. Decorative end-cut beams and rafters can be used in place of bracketing.

Pilasters, columns, or posts are possibilities for shade covers. Pilasters are plaster-finished squares with trim bases and caps. Columns can be pre-cast concrete in Classical or Tuscan detailing. If posts are used, they can be single or in twos or fours with decorative surrounds and corbel bracing, all finished in dark brown. Combination pilaster and post is possible using plaster or cut-stone veneering.

Water Features Design Concepts

Water Features

Traditional Italian water features are fountains with white marble art sculptures. For modern fountain designs, Italian walls create basins with Classical forms in plan view. Pools with natural color decorative concrete moldings also incorporate Classical forms. Fountains can have tall spray jets or tiered bowls with sculpted detailing.

Wall fountains can incorporate the Italian full arch form using natural color pre-cast concrete moldings. Wall fountains can have half-bowls or marble sculptures. Cut stone and marble are the best materials for vertical surfaces in wall fountains.

These water features at the Villa d'este in Rome are Italian originals. *Courtesy of Megan Flanagan.* *(continued on following page)*

The St. Regis has several fountains that demonstrate the integration of traditional Italian style into water feature design.

The Bellagio is also a good source for Italian water feature design ideas.

Fire Features Design Concepts

Fire Features

There are few fire features designed in Italian landscapes with true Italian features. The verticality of fireplaces allows an opportunity for a number of Italian features to be integrated. Chimneys can resemble the Italian Villa tower. Full arch forms can be incorporated into hearth and cabinet openings. Decorative trim for bases, caps, and belt courses can also be used. Counter, mantle, and hearth horizontal surfaces can be cut stone or poured-in-place concrete molding.

A traditional Italian fireplace at the St. Regis.

Seating Design Concepts

Seating

Permanent site furnishings for the Italian style are seatwalls with base and trim molding with plaster finishes. Caps can be pre-cast concrete molding. Chairs, benches, and tables can be natural color pre-cast concrete with molded edges. Decorative metal can also be used for furnishings. Soft, curving metal designs with a black finish are consistent with the style.

Some seating ideas from the St. Regis and the resorts of Las Vegas.

Planters

Permanent planters for the Italian are white or off-white plaster or cut stone with base and cap trim. Caps can also be natural color pre-cast concrete molding. Pots are white plaster castings of artistic urns and bowls. Intricate detailing can include grape leaves or sculpture designs.

Semi-formal planter designs at Palazzo in Las Vegas and the St. Regis.

Italian style pot at the Bellagio and the Palazzo.

Garden Art

The Italian style has a vast selection of garden art with Classical and Italian marble sculptures, decorative wrought iron designs, sundials, or vineyard design elements.

Garden art and paving examples from the St. Regis, the Bellagio, and the Palazzo.

PLANTING DESIGN

A direct descendant of Classical landscape design style is the Italian style. Though less formal, the Italian style has many conifers and is similarly shaped by the nation's Olive and Grape agriculture. Evergreens like Pinus pinea and Cupressus sempervirens are trees common for the Italian style. Italian cooking has popularized the herb garden with favorites like Rosmarinus officinalis and Thymus vulgaria, each which can actually be used as shrubs and groundcovers.

Many modern Italian landscape designs have morphed into the "Tuscan" style. For this style, a contrast of dark and light greens, dark purples, and silvers are used, with very few flowering shrubs. Instead, flowering vines are frequently used for color accents.

In California, winery buildings are surrounded by landscape designs that are reminiscent of the Italian style with elements of the Craftsman style.

This garden from Italy shows the common use of Cypresses and Pines in Italian planting design. *Courtesy of Judy Bradstreet.*

These planting design examples from The Village demonstrate the formal Italian style with Date Palm and Cypress colonnades and symmetrical, layered hedge rows. *(continued on following page)*

LEASING
LEASING

Plant Palette

Trees

Citrus sp.	Orange, Lemon, Kumquat
Cedrus deodora	Deodora cedar
Cedrus atlantica 'Glauca'	Blue Atlas Cedar
Cupressus sempervirens	Italian Cypress
Feijoa sellowiana	Pineapple Guava
Ficus carica	Edible Fig
Ficus sp.	Ornamental Fig
Ligustrum lucidum	Tree Privet
Olea europea	Olive
Pinus pinea	Italian Stone Pine
Prunus c.'Atropurpurea'	Purple-Leaf Plum

Shrubs

Arbutus unedo	Strawberry Tree
Callistemon 'Little John'	Dwarf Bottle Brush
Cerastium tomentosum	Dusty Miller
Cotoneaster sp.	Cotoneaster
Eleagnus pungens	Silverberry
Gardenia jasminoides	Gardenia
Grevillea 'Noellii'	Noel's Grevillea
Juniperus sp.	Juniper
Lavandula sp.	Lavender
Leptospermum sp.	Tea Tree
Ligustrum japonicum	Japanese Privet
Lirope muscari	Big Blue Lily Turf
Osmanthus fragrans	Sweet Olive
Pennisetum setaceum	Fountain Grass
Phormium tenax	New Zealand Flax
Pittosporum crassifolium	Willow-leaf Pittosporum
Pittosporum tobira	Mock Orange
Rhaphiolepis sp.	Indian Hawthorn
Rosa sp.	Rose
Rosmarinus officinallis	Rosemary

Vines and Espaliers

Jasminum polyanthum	Pink Jasmine
Lonicera japonica	Giant Honeysuckle
Mandevilla sp.	Mandevilla
Rosa sp.	Rose
Trachelospermum jasminoides	Star Jasmine
Wisteria sinensis	Chinese Wisteria

Groundcovers

Cissus rhombifolia	Grape Ivy
Festuca ovina 'Glauca'	Blue Fesue
Juniperus horizontalis	Spreading Juniper
Rosa sp.	Rose
Thymus vulgaria	Thyme
Trachelospermum jasminoides	Star Jasmine

Italian Planting Design

Planting Design Concept

Concept
Formal, symmetrical, manicured, vertical emphasis.

Trees
Large background mass: Pinus pinea (Italian Stone Pine)
Picturesque background: Prunus sp. (Flowering Cherry)
Columnar foreground evergreen: Cupressus sempervirens (Italian Cypress)
Small foreground accent: Citrus sinensis (Dwarf Citrus)

Shrubs
Background screen hedge: Podocarpus macrophyllus (Yew Pine)
Midground mass: Buxus microphylla japonica (Japanese Boxwood)
Pot accents: Ligustrum japonicum 'Columnar' (Columnar Privet) and Phormium tenax 'Tom Thumb' (Dwarf New Zealand Flax)

Groundcover
Foreground spreading: Juniperus horizontalis (Spreading Juniper) or Trachelospermum jasminoides (Star Jasmine)
Clumping foreground: Agapanthus africanus 'Peter Pan' (Dwarf Lily-of-the-Nile) or Lavandula sp. (Lavender)

This informal garden at the St. Regis shows palms, asymmetrical hedges, and border color.

Tuscan Planting Design

Planting Design Concept

Concept

Formal, symmetrical, and manicured use of contrasting dark greens, grays, purples, and bronzes.

Trees

Cedrus atlantica 'Glauca': Blue Atlas Cedar
Picturesque background canopy: Olea europea (Olive Tree)
Small midground accent: Prunus c. 'Atropurpurea' (Purple-leaf Plum) or Feijoa sellowiana (Pineapple Guava)
Columnar foreground evergreen: Cupressus sempervirens (Italian Cypress)

Shrubs

Background hedge: Ligustrum japonicum (Japanese Privet)
Midground hedge: Pittosporum crassifolium (Willow-leaf Pittosporum) or Eleagnus pungens (Silverberry)
Foreground hedge: Callistemon c. 'Little John' (Dwarf Bottlebrush)
Course foreground accent: Phormium tenax (New Zealand Flax)
Foreground spreading: Juniperus s. 'Tamariscifolia' (Tams Juniper) or Thymus vulgaria (Thyme)
Pot accents: Rosmarinus officinalis 'Columnar' (Columnar Rosemary) and Citrus sinensis (Dwarf Citrus)

Groundcover

Clumping foreground: Festuca ovina 'Glauca', Cerastium tomentosum (Dusty Miller), or Pennisetum setaceum (Purple Fountain Grass)
Foreground turf: Marathon Dwarf Fescue

Macaroni Grill in Oceanside, California, exhibits the Tuscan sub-style with a stone façade and a planting design featuring conifers.

Tuscan style planting design at Quail Hill in Irvine, California.

Chapter Seven
FRENCH

French • Rural French • French Colonial • Chateau • Chateauesque • Tudor Beaux-Arts • Elizabethan • French Revival • Normandy • Brittany • Creole

HISTORY

As with all styles of architecture, the French style began with geographical and climate-related influences. When French settlers came to America, they brought a style of construction that contributed to the design style. The three distinct features that have endured in all French-influenced architecture as it has evolved over time are a very steep roof, paired doors and windows with external shutters, and half-timber framing. The English were pre-disposed to designing from the outside in, but the French did the opposite, designing from the inside out. Having shutters open to the outside protected windows from strong winds. That is why we see shutters on the outside instead of in. We see large porches and verandahs in the French style because of the desire to be outside.

FRENCH COLONIAL

Architectural Design

During French occupation of the Louisiana Territory, buildings were connected with three primary features as a result of French climate influences. The areas with excessive rainfall and hurricanes had raised floors, supported by piers of up to two feet high. After the Louisiana Purchase, plantations became popular and raised floors were eventually covered with walls and converted into basements with exterior accesses. Another feature often found on southern plantations is the double-pitched hip roof. This is a result of extending the roofline to incorporate a verandah or four-sided porch (gallery). Also common during this era were exposed 90-degree rafter tails, full casement windows, and doors with glass transoms above. Some architecture was built without covering the half-timbering, leaving it exposed to the outside. This became a French distinction and a later identifying decorative element. Wood shingle roofs, decorative wrought iron door latches and hinges were used for doors and windows.

Distinctive Features

- Very steep roof with flared eaves
- Half timbering on walls
- Paired doors and windows with external shutters

SITE DESIGN

Feature Integration

Architectural features able to be translated into the landscape are the steep pitched roof, flared eaves, and verandahs for shade covers and arbor elements. Walls, fencing, trellises, and site furnishings can incorporate the concepts and patterns of half-timbering. The using of paired doors and external shutters are really building-specific characteristics, but the wood patterns created from these designs can be used for trellis, fence, and garden art designs. The decorative wrought iron hardware used for French Colonial architecture can also be repeated in site elements.

The French Colonial style features steep roofs, sometimes concave, double doors and windows, shutters, and dormers.

CHATEAU

Architectural Design

In 1885, Richard Morris Hunt's design of Chateaus started a revival of French Architecture. Chateaus were built as very elaborate, ornate castles based on Hunt's inspiration gained from Francis I's Chambord, Blois, and Chenonceaux. These designs commonly had a faux raised floor of uncoursed rock or rubblework and decorative half-timbering. The varied height, wood shingle roofs were very steep, often with flared eaves. The Chateaus were designed with massive stone chimneys, dormers, round arches, decorative cornices, and with string and belt courses. In some structures, smooth flat stone with narrow mortar joints was used, sometimes as quoins. The most elaborate of Chateaus have a strong emphasis on the vertical, with round turrets, pinnacles, spires, finials, copulas, and stacked multiple chimneys. The style is similar to the English as seen in the sub-styles "Normandy" and "Brittany."

Distinctive Features

- Irregular structure with round tower, steep roof, and flared eaves
- Vertically emphasized architectural elements
- Uncoursed rubblework

The buildings from France show the original use of half-timbering common to the Chateau sub-style. The original style was designed with a thatched roof, which would be rare to find in America because of fire building codes. *Courtesy of Todd and Judy Bradstreet and Tammi Strasen.*

SITE DESIGN

Feature Integration

A good Chateau landscape design would feature the traditional uncoursed rockwork and half-timber patterning for walls, fences, and trellises. Walls with cut stone can incorporate belt courses or quoins for added interest. Water and fire features can incorporate the rubblework into their designs, which would be similar to those found in the Cabin style, except with more angular and warm-colored rock. The Chateau provides many opportunities for a creative shade cover design. The use of flared eaves, cornices, round turrets, pinnacles, spires, finials, or copulas for a shade cover design will deliver that creativity.

The Chateau Bradbury in Duarte, California, shows several elements common to the Chateau style: a vertical structure with a steep-sloping roof and a turret.

CREOLE

Architectural Design

In the United States, the only remaining originally French-designed architecture is the Vieux Carre, in New Orleans, Louisiana. All others have disappeared and been replaced by new buildings. The French sub-style that replaced the original French designs is the "Creole," also seen primarily in New Orleans.

The Victorian Period Creole architecture has front-facing gable roofs with lacy cast-iron balconies, often with arches and hanging pots. Sometimes the Creole has an extended flat or low-pitched roof with decorative fascias and cornices in addition to the decorative railing.

Distinctive Features

- Front-facing gable roof
- Lacy cast-iron balcony
- Sometimes decorative fascias or cornices

The most distinguishing feature of the Creole style is the *gallerie* with very ornate ironwork posts, railings, and arches. The Gingerbread Bed and Breakfast in Cape May, New Jersey, demonstrates this feature. *Courtesy of the Gingerbread Bed and Breakfast.*

SITE DESIGN

Feature Integration

The main design element that clearly distinguishes the Creole from any other style is the lacy cast-iron balcony. This element repeated in fencing, trellises, or site furnishings clearly communicates the style.

The Mansard is an unmistakable sub-style with a dormered roof that is virtually the top floor of a building.

A very ornate French style building, the Kimberly-Crest House in Redlands, California, combines the steep roof and coned turrets of the Chateau with Second Empire cresting and some Classical elements.

French Forms

Materials and Finishes

Concrete is not normally used in French construction, but if it is used, it should include warm colors. For both the French Colonial and the Chateau, rough-sawn lumber framing is used to demonstrate the half-timbering. The lumber is painted in dark brown, with smooth plaster for wall surfacing. French Colonial walls are usually yellow; Chateau colors are off-white to tan.

French stone for walls is normally cut quarry stone blocks with warm-colored or a varied brownish tinting. Paving is warm-colored random or cut stone. Steel is used mainly for ornamentation. Both the French Colonial and the Creole feature decorative wrought iron, which is normally finished in glossy black.

Color Palette

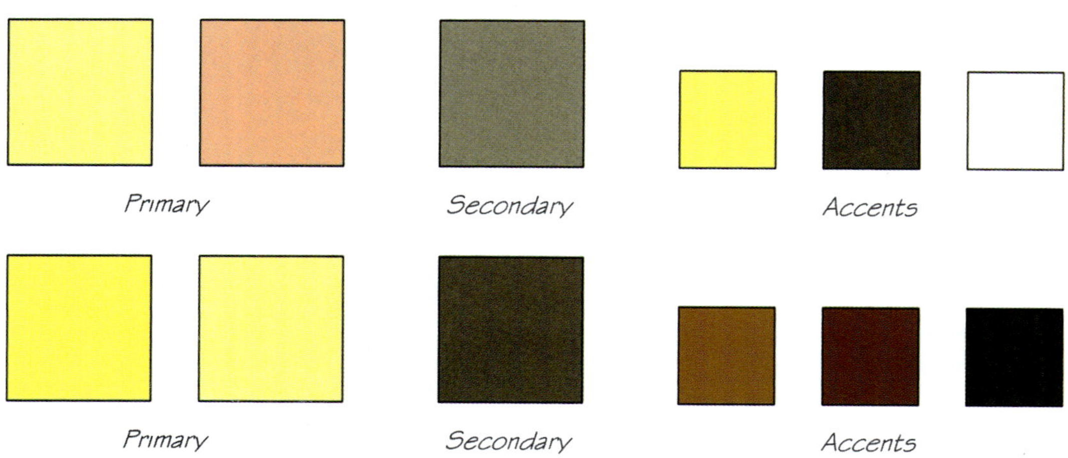

Paving Design Concepts

Paving

Hardscape layout is informal and organic for French design (the Second Empire style is really the formal French style). Paving is designed in plan view with freeform, meandering walkways and stone-paved landings. For the French Colonial, random stone paving provides the rural look, while ashlar patterned cut stone matches the Chateau theme. Colonial steps and stepping-stones are random stone. Chateau steps and stepping pads are cut stone. Treads can have a cantilevered stone nose for added detail.

Irregular patterned stone paving or brick patterns are common to the French Colonial and the Chateau. Courtesy of the *Country French Bed and Breakfast in Lafayette, Louisiana.* *(continued on following page)*

Wall Design Concepts

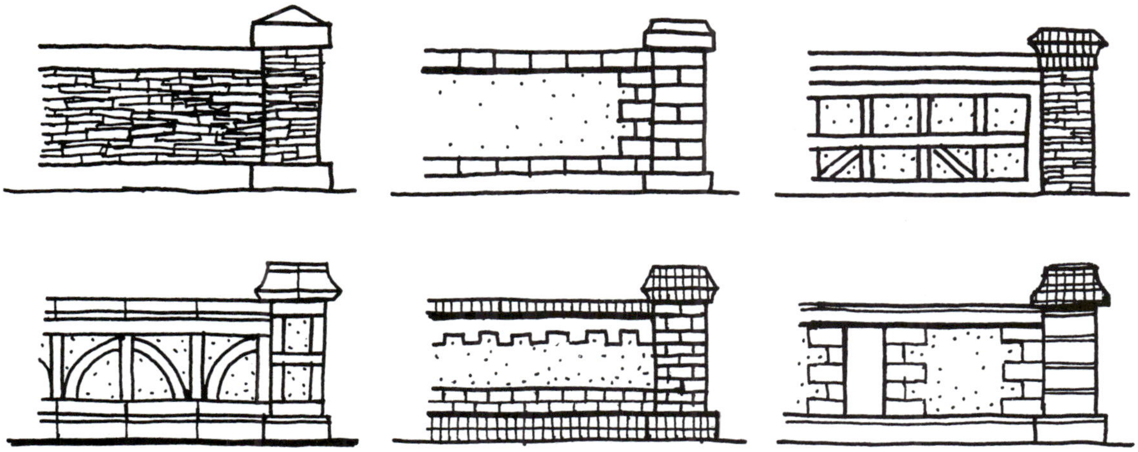

Walls

Where weather permits, the traditional design for French walls is with half-timbering stick work. This would be with rough-cut lumber and a smooth plaster finish. Wall caps would also be wood.

For more sturdy walls, the French Colonial would have warm-colored round rock with or without mortar. The Chateau would have stacked angular or cut stone blocks (also warm-colored), either with small grout joints or without them at all. A nice touch for Chateau walls would be to provide a lumber-framed half-timber wall with stone pilasters.

Masonry French structures incorporate used brick and stone materials, which can be repeated into site walls.
Courtesy of Todd and Judy Bradstreet.

Walls designed for the Chateau sub-style are earth-tone quarry stone. Walls can incorporate quoins or stone around archways.

Materials for formal French and Mansard design are likely to be finished masonry with quoins and decorative capping. *Courtesy of Jerri Pick.*

Fence Design Concepts

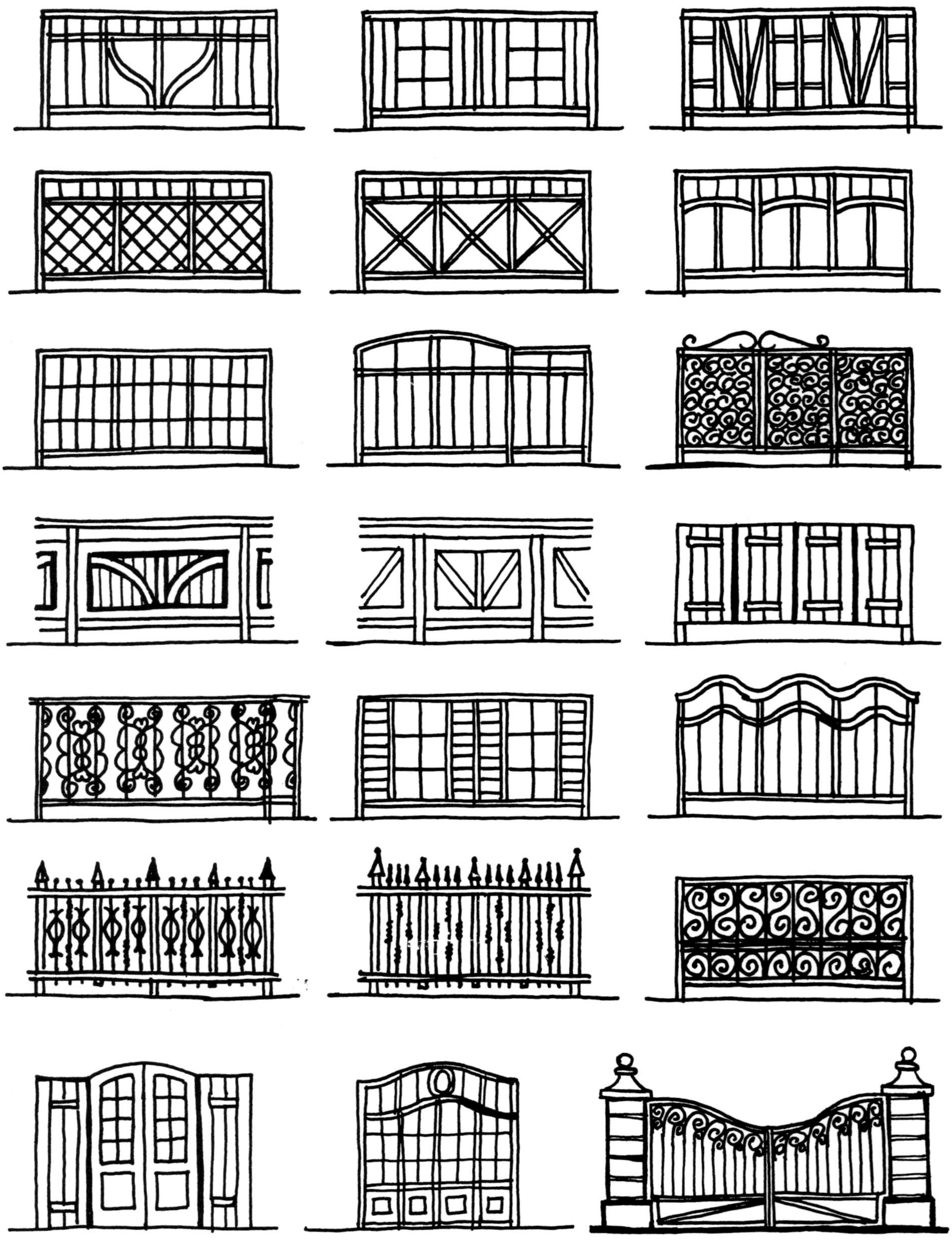

Fences

For both solid and open Colonial wood fencing, designs would be simple, unfinished rough-cut (or even split) vertical slat with pointed ends. The Colonial could incorporate the double door and shutter design forms for wood fencing. The Chateau's solid fencing would be half-timbered walls. For open fences, designs can embrace the half-timbering patterns, similar to the Victorian Stick.

For the Creole, and also for the Colonial, wrought iron fencing can be used. The most extreme ornamentation can be used for French steel fencing. Posts have finials and pickets have spear tops. Creole fencing usually has patterns of double verticals with lacing or flower designs between. Where gates are desired, the Creole full arch should be used. Many French entryways feature some type of fancy ornamental wrought iron design finished in black.

French design uses decorative wrought iron fencing, normally painted black. When wood fencing is used, it is normally in the form of spaced milled pickets, either white or unfinished.

This *gallerie* can provide inspiration for Creole fencing.

Trellises

Similar to fencing, trellises can be wood or steel for the French style. The Chateau would likely incorporate half-timber patterning to trellis design. French Colonial and Creole designs are likely to be ornamental wrought iron with lacy detailing. A Creole trellis would have two panels of double verticals with lacy inset separated by an intricate detailing where vines can twine. Like the Italian style, French trellis design includes the design of grape arbors.

A French arbor supporting a rose vine in a very colorful, informal garden and another supporting a Ficus pumila vine.

Shade Cover Design Concepts

Shade Covers

The variation of materials and design forms provides many opportunities for French style shade covers. Both solid and open Colonial wood shade covers can incorporate the steep roof and overhanging curved eaves. Supporting structures can be all wood posts or pilasters, which incorporate French materials like warm-colored stone and quoins.

Chateau shade covers can incorporate the half-timbering into Stick-like designs with crossing trusses, but with steep roof and curved eaves. Supporting structures for the Chateau are large, square full-height pilasters with cut block stone veneer and stone caps. The signature Chateau copulas and finials can be included for a finishing touch.

Other possibilities can be grape arbors or gazebos created from lacy wrought iron, finished in black. Spires and pinnacles can top these elements.

This Chateauesque shade cover from Classic Design Systems shows a step roof with exposed trussing and quarry stone pilasters. *Courtesy of Classic Design Systems.*

Water Features Design Concepts

Water Features

Traditional French water features are grand basins with finely detailed sculptures and bowls as can be seen in Paris. These fountains are more appropriate with formal Second Empire designs, but can be scaled down for French Colonial or the Chateau. Rural French water features would be round rock basins and plaster birdbaths. Depending on the scale of the project, traditional French fountain elements can be repeated in smaller, but still fine-detailed designs.

Fire Features Design Concepts

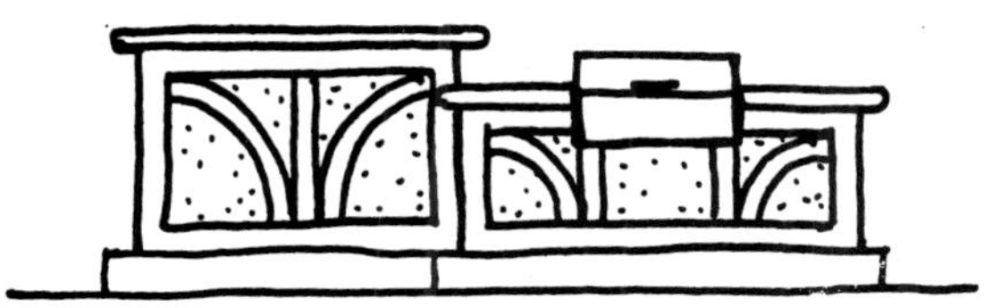

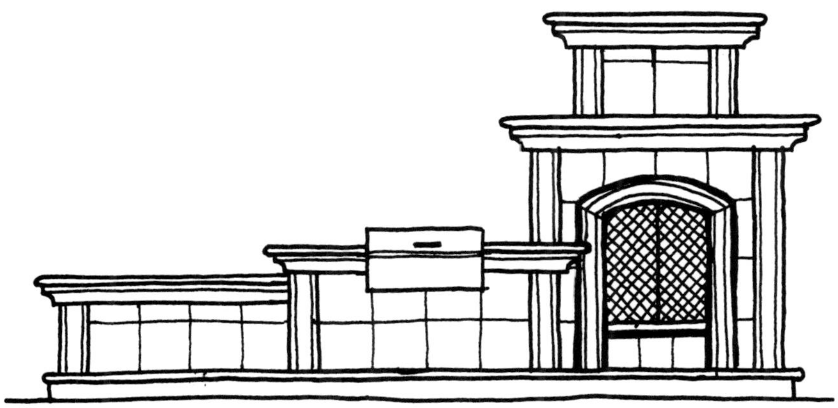

Fire Features

Fire features for the French Colonial are going to be similar to the Ranch and Cabin styles with stacked round rock, except with warm coloring. Door openings can reflect the wood shutter design. For the Chateau, fireplaces feature massive uses of large warm-colored cut block stones. Door openings for barbeques and fireplaces are fine-detailed decorative wrought iron finished in black. For special decoration, copulas, pinnacles, or spires can be placed on chimneystacks.

This French fireplace has the form of a Mansard roof, but is constructed with irregular stone, creating a Chateauesque look.

Seating Design Concepts

Seating

Portable French seating can vary greatly. Colonial design would be unfinished, rough cut lumber. However, along with the Creole, it can also be 100% ornamental wrought iron with all detailed lacing. This can be with either a white or black finish. For the Chateau, wood site furnishings with half-timbering patterns would be consistent with the style. Stone benches would be used as permanent seating.

Planter Design Concepts

Planters

French detailing opens opportunities for planters. Permanent planters would be constructed from warm-colored stone or would be wood-framed construction with half-timbering patterns and pot liners inside. For pots, French design is what we see in water feature statuary. It is highly detailed white marble or plaster castings. Designs are typically white bowls or inverted bell shapes with decorative lace and grape vine detailing.

Garden Art

Traditional French garden art is white marble statuary. French artists from the Renaissance created many of the statues found in France and inspired in the United States. Lacy detailing is found on urns, birdbaths, and sculptures. For French Colonial design, garden art is more natural with warm colors replacing the whites. Birdhouses and decorative wrought iron features might be found.

French site furnishings, planters, and garden art are ornate with fine detailing. *Courtesy of Todd and Judy Bradstreet.*

Planting Design

The French are well known for their artistic flair, which can also be in their landscape designs. French country gardens are very informal, almost with an organized, wild look. One would normally find bright, fine textured foliage with an almost lacy look. A profusion of dainty, colorful flowers that can be cut and brought inside to brighten a room are indicative of the French garden. The variety of color both in foliage and flower creates a soft and inviting space. Plants characteristic of the French style are Abelia grandiflora, Diosma pulchrum, Felicia amelloides, and Lavandula.

Examples of informal French Country gardens showing vines, profuse color, asymmetrical design layout, and natural groupings.

2462

In America, the Chateau style planting design is similar to the Cabin, using conifers and cold-climate plant material. Since French Chateaus are normally tall, and steep roofed, tall trees need to reflect this look. Use of Pines, Cedars, and Maples for the sky plane and native deciduous shrubs and groundcovers on the ground plane can achieve this. For the Chateau, the vertical is emphasized with tall trees. Beneath is an understory ground plane that gives the landscape a pedestrian scale.

Much of the Formal French planting design is projected into the landscape through Mansard architectural forms. The symmetrical layout and use of quoins is translated into the landscape with hedges and topiaries. This can clearly be seen in Second Empire style gardens. For further elaboration, see chapter eight.

Formal French gardens include hedging, topiaries, and symmetrical layout. *Courtesy of Jerri Pick.*

Although mostly formal, the garden design at the Vaux-le-Vicomte in Maincy, Melun, France, has colorful, informal wildflower beds. *Courtesy of Todd and Judy Bradstreet.*

Plant Palette

Trees

Bauhinia purpurea	Orchid Tree
Betula pendula	White Birch
Cinnamomum camphora	Camphor Tree
Gleditsia triacanthos	Honey Locust
Jacaranda mimosifolia	Jacaranda
Laburnum sp.	Golden Chain Tree
Lagerstroemia indica	Crape Myrtle
Liriodendron tulipfera	Tulip Tree
Magnolia sp.	Magnolia
Pyrus calleryana	Ornamental Pear
Robinia pseudoacacia	Black Locust
Tabebuia sp.	Trumpet Tree

Shrubs

Asparagus sp.	Asparagus
Abelia grandiflora	Glossy Abelia
Arbutus unedo	Strawberry Tree
Azalea indica	Azalea
Buddleja davidii	Butterfly Bush
Calluna vulgaris	Scotch Heather
Camellia japonica	Camellia
Chamelacium uncinatum	Waxflower
Coprosma kirkii	Mirror Shrub
Cuphea hyssopifolia	Mexican Heather
Diosma pulchrum	Pink Breath of Heaven
Digitalis sp.	Monkey Flower
Euryops sp.	Bush Daisy
Erica sp.	Heather
Escallonia sp.	Pink Princess
Felicia amelloides	Blue Marguerite
Fuschia hybrida	Fuschia
Gardenia jasminoides	Gardenia
Hebe sp.	False Heather
Hemerocallis sp.	Daylily
Iris germanica	Bearded Iris
Lathyrus sp.	Sweet Pea
Lavandula denata	French Lavender
Leptospermum sp.	Tea Tree
Ligustrum japonicum	Japanese Privet
Myrtus communis	Common Myrtle
Nandina domestica	Heavenly Bamboo
Rosa sp.	Rose
Rosmarius officianalis	Rosemary
Syringa vulgaris	Common Lilac
Thymus vulgaria	Thyme
Veronica sp.	Heather
Viburnum sp.	Viburnum

Vines and Espaliers

Bignonia violacea	Purple Trumpet Vine
Ipomoea sp.	Morning Glory
Jaminum polyanthum	Pink Jasmine
Jasminum humile	Italian Jasmine
Solanum jasminoides	White Potato Vine

Groundcovers

Alcea rosea	Hollyhock
Convolvulus cneorum	Bush Morning Glory
Cosmos	
Osteospermum fruticosum	African Daisy
Papaver sp.	Poppy
Wildflowers	

Planting Design Concept

French Country Planting Design

Concept
Informal, asymmetrical, and natural use of fine textures, light greens, and colorful but delicate flowers.

Trees
Large background mass: Pinus mugo (European Pine)
Midground evergreen: Cinnamomum camphora (Camphor Tree)
Midground deciduous: Robinia pseudoacacia (Black Locust)
Midground vertical accent: Betula pendula (European White Birch)
Small flowering midground: Magnolia soulangeana (Saucer Magnolia)
Small foreground accent: Camellia japonica (Camellia)

Shrubs
Background mass: Buddleja davidii (Butterfly Bush) and Escallonia sp. (Pink Princess)
Midground masses: Leptospermum sp. (Tea Tree), Rosmarinus officinalis (Rosemary), Abelia grandiflora (Glossy Abelia), and Diosma pulchrum (Pink Breath of Heaven)
Foreground masses: Hemerocallis sp. (Daylily) and Felicia amelloides (Blue Marguerite)
Foreground mound: Euryops sp. (Bush Daisy)

Groundcover
Clumping foreground: Azalea indica (Southern Azalea), Lavandula sp. (Lavender), and Cuphea hyssopifolia (Mexican Heather)
Foreground turf: Festuca sp. (Dwarf Fescue)

Chapter Eight

SECOND EMPIRE

Second Empire • Mansard • French Eclectic

HISTORY

A French style so distinct from others that it needs its own mention is the Second Empire, which is easily identified by its mansard roof. Napoleon III of France ruled from 1848 to 1857, at which time he implemented a remodel of the Louvre, which led to a complete overhaul of the architectural style for France. The new style was to make use of the upper floor attic area by expanding the roof to the sides of the structure into what is a "Mansard" roof, named for its founder, architect Francois Mansart. The Second Empire style came to America at the beginning of the Victorian Period and flourished from 1860 to 1880.

In 1960, there was a Revival of the Second Empire, but without all the Victorian accoutrements. The style was simply the "Mansard," because it took normal symmetrical rectangular buildings and added mansard roofs with dormers. Often, minor decorative French elements were used like quoins, louvered shutters, and paired doors.

The average individual would say they have never heard of the Second Empire style. If they saw Second Empire architecture, they would immediately associate it with that of a haunted house. Two well-known "haunted" houses are Psycho House at Universal Studios and the Addams Family House.

The Second Empire style is inspired by the French. The Vaux-le-Vicomte in Maincy, Melun, France, has all the features inherent to Second Empire: steep mansard roofs, quoins, and fine ornamentation and detailing. The site layout is very formal. Architect Louis le Vau and landscape architect Andre le Notre joined forces to create this design wonder. *Courtesy of Todd, Judy, and Vickie Bradstreet.*

Architectural Design

The Second Empire style is very ornate and grandiose with its signature mansard roof, frequently with pedimented dormers and a pattern of slate shingles. The roof is actually a dual-pitch hipped design with molding at every edge and transition of roofline. On top of the roof is usually ironwork cresting and under the eaves, decorative bracketing.

There are six types of Mansard roofs. The three most common are the straight, the flared, and the concave. Convex s-curve and reverse s-curve mansards are less common.

Most buildings are symmetrical with the center as the focus of visual interest. At the center, square towers or pavilions and copulas project skyward. Projecting forward at the front entry is a very ornate veranda. Front doors are in pairs and windows are typically 2 over 2 double-hung with hooding, molding, and louvered shutters.

Distinctive Features

- Symmetrical structure with square tower
- Mansard roof with hooded dormers, ironwork cresting, and bracketing
- Very ornate veranda

In these Second Empire close-ups, notice the fine detailing of the walls, quoins, roof cresting, corner finials, and chimneys. *Courtesy of Tammi Strasen.*

SITE DESIGN

Feature Integration

The formality of the Second Empire is transferred into the landscape using symmetrical blocks and repetition of form in site planning. The purpose of Second Empire design was to provide a royal appearance to buildings. It is important to keep in mind, every site and landscape element needs to be formally placed, and able to be cleanly maintained.

This style flourished at the beginning of the Victorian Era, which is why the design and materials used in the Mansard roofs is similar to the Queen Anne building façades. Like the Queen Anne, the Empire uses trim-framed shingle patterns. However, the Empire normally uses hard materials for walls with the decorative shingle patterning for the roof. The Second Empire also uses ironwork detailing instead of wood scrolling. The shingles and ironwork are elements that are able to be integrated into the landscape. Mansard towers and copulas can be reflected into shade structures. The other French-influenced elements: double doors, shutters, and quoins can be repeated in fences and walls.

The clock towers at the House of Parliament, England, and Philadelphia Town Hall, Pennsylvania, demonstrate the verticality and ornamentation Second Empire can assume. The towers have dual-tiered mansard roofs with finials at every roof intersection. *Courtesy of Todd and Judy Bradstreet.*

Though its towers are clearly Gothic, the Notre Dame Cathedral building is considered by many to be Second Empire because of its detailing. *Courtesy of Tammi Strasen.*

Second Empire architecture can be found in most of the one-time English-controlled provinces and countries like the Hotel Windsor in Melbourne, Australia. *Courtesy of the Hotel Windsor.*

Inspired by the French occupation of the Louisiana Territory, Second Empire architecture has appeared on many public buildings in the South. These courthouses from the Texas counties of Parker, Laredo, Goliad, Concho, Presidio, and Shackleford are incredible examples of Second Empire style, each with different mansard types and exterior colors. *Courtesy of Bob Weston.* *(continued on following 3 pages)*

1886

Second Empire Forms

Materials and Finishes

The primary materials to be used in site landscape design are colored brick and the signature wood shingles from the Mansard roof with 1x4 and 1x6 trim framing. As with the Queen Anne, the finishing is normally a palette of feminine colors. However, the colors are typically more brilliant and more varied.

Also bright colored are the Second Empire masonry walls that, along with quoins, may be repeated in site masonry design. Walls are constructed with colored brick or smooth surfacing. The color palette is normally three distinct hues with a primary wall color, a light color for quoins and trim, and a dark color for the roof.

Ironwork cresting can be repeated for highly ornamented wrought iron fencing, normally black, but can also be white. Stone and organic materials are not used in the formal design of the Second Empire.

The architecture of Main Street at Disneyland in Anaheim, California, was designed with a variety of Second Empire concepts. *(continued on following 3 pages)*

CITY HALL
DEPOT MAIN STREET PLAZA

BOOK
GIFTS
101
101

Blue Ribbon
Bakery
Coffee & Baked
Blue Ribbon Bakery

Plaza Inn

Two examples of Second Empire style for residential use are the Ocean House in Carlsbad (below), California, and the Morey Mansion in Redlands (left), California, both with complex mansard roof structures.

Color Palette

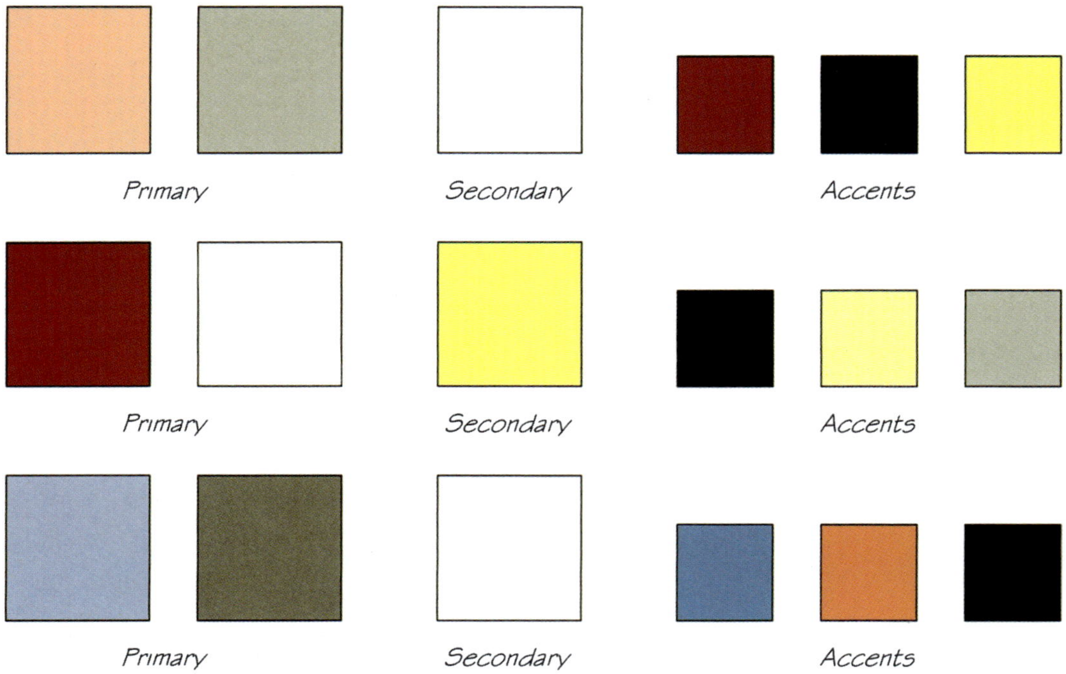

Paving Design Concepts

Paving

The multitude of materials and finishes used in the Second Empire create many opportunities for paving design. Like the Queen Anne, the decorative shingle patterns can be integrated into walkways and decks using concrete pavers with natural concrete banding. In addition, wall materials like colored brick and concrete can be used to repeat the decorative patterning.

Whatever the material, the paving design must be laid in formal symmetry. Since the Second Empire normally has a central focal element like a tower or protruding verandah, a straight central walkway is needed to further direct focus on the central building element. Where steps are needed, concrete banding or colored brick can be used.

Hardscape for Second Empire would normally be formal, like this paving at the Kimberly-Crest House in Redlands, California. Residential hardscape would be the same as Victorian style.

Wall Design Concepts

Walls

Second Empire walls are designed with formal rectangular geometrics. Consistent design would use quoins at edges, corners, and pilasters. Pilaster caps can reflect mansard roof design. Walls are smooth masonry. Where brick veneer is used, grout joints should be flush or slightly tooled. Otherwise a colored smooth plaster finish is consistent with the style.

Fence Design Concepts

Fences

Fence design for the Empire uses highly ornamented wrought iron to follow the ironwork cresting. Another good source of inspiration for fencing design is Creole style balcony ironwork. The wrought iron design can be augmented with masonry pilasters.

Trellis Design Concepts

Trellises

Trellis design is also with decorative wrought iron.

Shade Cover Design Concepts

Shade Covers

By far, the opportunities to create the most extremely ornate arbors or gazebos are generated by the Second Empire elements, forms, materials, and colors. A formal Second Empire gazebo should feature symmetrical design with a mansard roof topped by a central mansard copula and edged with cresting. Gazebos and shade structures follow the square or octagonal design. Posts and pickets can be wood, but more closely follow the style with wrought iron detailing.

This copula in France shows possible inspiration for a Second Empire gazebo. *Courtesy of Todd and Judy Bradstreet.*

Water Feature Design Concepts

Water Features

To design water features in the Second Empire style, one approach would be to use the mansard roof forms. However, when the style was first introduced in France, fountains were designed for the formal gardens. Using these French fountains as inspiration would be the traditional way to design a Second Empire fountain. The traditional Second Empire fountain is natural concrete with very ornate forms and detailing. Basins can be quatrefoil or other complex geometric forms. Instead of tiers of smaller bowls, internal features are sculptures of humans, animals, fish, or other detailed focal points.

A French fountain in Las Vegas, Nevada, demonstrating a Second Empire flavor.

Fire Feature Design Concepts

Fire Features

While there are many examples of Second Empire fountains, there are few examples of fireplaces or other fire features. To remain consistent with the style, fire features need to be formal in symmetry. Masonry construction allows an opportunity to incorporate quoins and decorative veneer patterns.

Seating

Permanent seating for the Second Empire is brick construction. For portable seating, benches and tables can be designed either like the Queen Anne with shingle patterning for back rests or with ornamental wrought iron with maximum detailing.

Planters

Permanent planters are similar to permanent seating, composed of brick with veneer patterning. Pots are highly detailed cast plaster or concrete with sculpted grapes, leaves, or other French elements.

Garden Art

For garden art, urns and French sculptures can be used. Art is highly decorative, but placement in the site is a formal, symmetrical layout.

The Garden at Versailles is a formal landscape with many examples of garden art like this decorative urn atop a Classical pedestal. *Courtesy of Todd and Judy Bradstreet.*

A formal annual color bed at the Queen Victoria Inn in Cape May, New Jersey. *Courtesy of the Queen Victoria Inn Bed and Breakfast.*

Planting Design

The Second Empire planting design is really what we know as Formal French garden design. It is a combination of the English, French Country, and Victorian garden styles: a very formal manicured garden with geometric formed pockets of colorful flowers. Nearly every shrub is hedged or topiaried. All flowerbeds are bordered with hedgerows.

This aerial view of Paris from atop the Effiel Tower shows the very formal site layout of both buildings and landscape. *Courtesy of Tammi Strasen.*

Plant Palette

Trees

Bauhinia purpurea	Orchid Tree
Betula pendula	White Birch
Cedrus atlantica 'Glauca'	Blue Atlas Cedar
Citrus sinensis	Citrus
Cupressus sempervirens	Italian Cypress
Ginkgo biloba	Ginkgo
Jacaranda mimosifolia	Jacaranda
Juniperus sp.	Vertical Juniper
Liquidambar styraciflua	Sweet Gum
Pinus sp.	Pine
Pittosporum sp.	Pittosporum
Platanus acerifolia	London Plane Tree
Populus sp.	Poplar
Prunus sp.	Flowering Cherry
Pyrus calleryana	Ornamental Pear
Quercus sp.	Oak

Shrubs

Azalea indica	Southern Azalea
Buddleja davidii	Butterfly Bush
Buxus japonica	Japanese Boxwood
Calluna vulgaris	Scotch Heather
Coprosma kirkii	Mirror Shrub
Cuphea hyssopifolia	Mexican Heather
Diosma pulchrum	Pink Breath of Heaven
Digitalis sp.	Foxglove
Euonymus sp.	ncn
Euryops sp.	Bush Daisy
Erica sp.	Heather
Felicia amelloides	Blue Marguerite
Hebe sp.	False Heather
Hemerocallis hybrids	Daylily
Iris germanica	Bearded Iris
Lavandula denata	French Lavender
Ligustrum japonicum	Japanese Privet
Myrtus communis	Common Myrtle
Rhaphiolepis indica	Indian Hawthorn
Rosa sp.	Rose
Rosmarius officianalis	Rosemary
Spiraea sp.	Spiraea
Stachys sp.	Snowbell
Taxus baccata	English Yew
Thymus vulgaria	Thyme

Vines and Espaliers

Bignonia violacea	Purple Trumpet Vine
Jaminum polyanthum	Pink Jasmine
Jasminum humile	Italian Jasmine
Pandorea sp.	Bower Vine
Solanum jasminoides	White Potato Vine

Groundcovers

Cosmos sp.	Cosmos
Osteospermum fruticosum	African Daisy
Papaver sp.	Poppy

Planting Design Concept

Second Empire Planting Design

Concept
Very formal, symmetrical, very manicured, contrasting hedge form and color emphasis.

Trees
Large background mass: Pinus pinea (Italian Stone Pine)
Large background deciduous: Jacaranda mimosifolia (Jacaranda)
Midground vertical specimen: Pyrus calleryana (Ornamental Pear)
Small foreground accent: Citrus sinensis (Dwarf Citrus)

Shrubs
Background hedge: Pittosporum sp. (Pittosporum)
Midground hedge: Rosmarinus officinalis (Rosemary)
Foreground hedge: Myrtus communis (Common Myrtle)
Midground vertical accent: Taxus baccata (English Yew)
Pot topiary: Ligustrum japonicum (Japanese Privet)
Flowering foreground: Azalea indica (Southern Azalea)

Groundcover
Foreground turf: Festuca sp. (Dwarf Fescue)

A view of the formal Garden at the Vaux-le-Vicomte with symmetry, repetition of forms, manicured planting, and maze hedges. *Courtesy of Vickie Bradstreet.*

Glossary

Arch, full: a half circle arch with tangent side intersections.

Arch, lancet: a pointed arch, common to Gothic architecture.

Arch, segmented: an arch with non-tangent side intersections.

Balustrade: a barrier created by a linear series of bollards, normally seen as decorative concrete in Classical architecture.

Batter: the slight angle on a dry-stacked wall, wide at the bottom and narrow at the top.

Board and batten: vertical wood siding with narrow "battens" placed over the seams of wide "boards," common to Gothic and Ranch architecture.

Battlement: the up and down stepping on the top edge of Medieval towers.

Belt course: a projecting masonry course at the mid-level of a second or multi-story building, common to Italian architecture.

Board on board: even sized and spaced vertical wood siding with the one layer of boards covering the spacing in the bottom layer of boards with a slight overlap.

Box and strip: see *board and batten*

Bracketing: decorative bracing supporting the eaves of a roof against a wall, common to Italian and Second Empire architecture.

Cantilever: an over-hanging floor or beam extension beyond the supporting wall or post.

Capital: in Classical architecture, the horizontal element appearing like crown molding that rests on the top of columns. The pediment sits on top of the capital.

Castellation: an ornate castle finial.

Clapboard: horizontal wood siding, also known as weatherboard.

Corbel: a small decorative brace between a post and beam.

Chinking: clay packing between the gaps in log cabin walls.

Column order: the various types of Classical columns: Corinthian, Doric, Greek, Ionic, Roman; See Chapter One.

Copula: A decorative miniature version of the tower or gazebo on which it resides.

Cornice: crown molding on the outside of a structure.

Cresting: the ironwork on the top of a roof, common to Second Empire architecture.

Dentils: square teeth-like ornamentation just below a roof line, common to Georgian architecture.

Dormer: a window projection through a sloping roof.

Entablature: decorative notching and scripting in a capital.

Finial: a normally pointed ornate feature at the high point of a roof or on top of a post or picket.

Fluting: vertical routing in a Classical column.

Half-timbering: a technique common to French Chateau architecture where lumber is left exposed with wattle and daub filled in between.

Hewing (Hewn): in Log Cabin architecture, a technique where the bark is removed from logs and then the logs are cut flat on the top and bottom so they can be stacked.

Knee-brace: similar to bracketing, a brace that supports a beam extended beyond a wall, common to Craftsman architecture.

Lintel: a load-bearing beam which spans a door or window opening.

Loggia: a pillared porch with a least one side open.

Muntins: the pieces dividing the sections of glass in a window.

Nogging: the brick infilling between the timbers of a timber-framed building.

Mortise and tenon: The method used for connecting large structural lumber (usually post and beam) prior to the advent of metal ties, common in Early American architecture. The mortise is a cavity and the tenon is a carved end piece that fits inside the mortise.

Mullion: the vertical sides of a window sash.

Parapet: a wall extension above the roof line.

Pediment: in Classical architecture, a large triangular feature with decorative facing installed on top of a capital to support a gable roof.

Picket: the vertical members of a fence that create the barrier.
Pilaster: a short column.
Pinnacle: similar to a finial, an ornate feature at the high point of a roof or on top.
Plant-on: vertical wood trim applied on four sides of a column or post.
Plinth: a column base, common to Classical architecture.
Porte cochere: a covered car port connected to the main building.
Portico: a roofed entrance flanked by columns.
Quoins: large masonry-like projections on the corner edges of a building, common to French and Second Empire architecture.
Rafter tail: Rafter extensions beyond the edge of eaves with decorative end cuts.
Roof, flared: a steep roof or a concave roof with curved eaves.
Roof, gable: the most simple roof with two opposing sloping sides, common to Early American and Cabin architecture.
Roof, gambrel: a dual pitched gable roof common in Cape Cod, Barn architecture.
Roof, hipped: a roof with four sloping sides.
Roof, mansard: a dual-pitched hipped roof, common to Second Empire architecture.
Roof, shed: a roof with one sloping side.
Saltbox: The first Early American dwelling, a simple all lumber four-sided structure with a steep gable roof.
Scrolling: Script-like decorative wood edging installed under eaves and at post tops.
Spindlework: lathe-turned posts, pickets, and other decorative wood elements normally used for porches, turrets, and gazebos, common to Queen Anne architecture.
Stickwork: a decorative design layout of lumber installed over standard clapboard siding or on guardrails, common to Stick and Swiss Chalet architecture.
Surround: horizontal wood trim applied around a column or post.
Tracery: the decorative pattern of supporting mullions, common to Gothic architecture.
Turret: a tower element normally with a steep, pointed roof.
Tympanum: the decorative area inside the molding of a pediment.
Veneer: the face of a wall.
Verandah: a covered porch.
Vergeboard: lace-like decorative woodwork installed under eaves, common to Medieval architecture.
Wattle and daub: a mixture of clay and straw used to pack between half-timbering.
Weatherboard: see *clapboard*.

Bibliography

Adams, Denise Wiles. *Restoring American Gardens: an Encyclopedia of Heirloom and Ornamental Plants 1640-1940.* Portland, Oregon: Timber Press, Inc., 2004.

Baker, John Milnes. *American House Styles: a Concise Guide.* New York, New York: W.W. Norton & Company, Inc., 1994.

Buchholz, Barbara and Lisa Skolnik. *French Country*. New York, New York: Michael Friedman Publishing Group, Inc., 1996.

Carley, Rachael. *The Visual Dictionary of American Domestic Architecture*. New York, New York: Roundtable Press Inc., 1994.

De Luz, Jan. *The French Touch*. Salt Lake City, Utah: Gibbs, Smith Publisher, 2004.

Downing, Andrew Jackson. *A Treatise on the Theory and Practice of Landscape Gardening.* Washington, D.C.: Dumbarton Oaks Trustees of Harvard University, 1991.

Downing, Andrew Jackson. *The Architecture of Country Houses*. New York, New York: Dover Publications, Inc., 1969.

Downing, Andrew Jackson. *Victorian Cottage Residences*. New York, New York: Dover Publications, Inc., 1981.

Foley, Roger. *Washington's Gardens at Mount Vernon: Landscape of an Inner Man.* New York, New York: Houghton Mifflin Company, 1999.

Gupton, Oscar W. and Fred C. Swope. *Trees and Shrubs of Virginia.* Charlottesville, Virginia: University Press of Virginia, 1981.

Jablonski, Ramona. *The Medieval Garden Design Book*. Owings Mills, Maryland: Stemmer House Publishers, 1982.

Jennings, Anne. *Georgian Gardens*. London, England: English Heritage, 2005.

McAlester, Virginia and Lee. *A Field Guide of American Houses.* New York, New York: Alfred A. Knopf, Inc., 2004.

Perry, Robert. *Landscape Plants for Western Regions*. Claremont, California: Land Design Publishing, 1992.

Ryley, Claire. *Roman Gardens and Their Plants.* Lewes, Sussex: Sussex Achaeological Society.

Stalley, Roger. *Early Medieval Architecture.* Oxford, England: Oxford University Press, 1999.

Sunset Publishing Corporation Editorial Staff. *Sunset Western Garden Book.* Menlo Park, California: Sunset Publishing Corporation, 2006.

Taylor, Patrick. *One Hundred English Gardens.* New York, New York: Rizzoli International Publications, Inc., 1996.

Viette, Andre and Mark. *Mid-Atlantic Gardener's Guide.* Nashville, Tennessee: Cool Springs Press, 2003.

Weishan, Michael and Cristina Roig. *From a Victorian Garden: Creating the Romance of a Bygone Age Right in Your Own Backyard.* New York, New York: The Penguin Group, 2004.

A Message From the Author

Southern California has a wonderful climate, varying topography, and many native plant zones, all in a relatively small region. Only in Southern California can one ski and surf in the same day. It's possible to drive along the coast, over the hilly oak woodlands, through the desert, and to the forested mountains within only a few hours time. The result is an opportunity for almost any style of architecture and landscape design.

A life-long resident of Southern California, currently residing in Orange County, I have been fortunate to experience all this region has to offer. Orange County is the land of opportunity for landscape architectural design, rich in high quality firms. I have been fortunate to work for, with, and among some of the best landscape architects in the world. Many of the examples and ideas in this book have come from or are inspirations from this great area of the country.

When I was a student of landscape architecture at Cal Poly, Pomona, I had no idea how blessed I was to have the instructors who were on staff at the time. Recognizable names like Francis Dean, John Lyle, and Bob Perry were only three in an all-star lineup that comprised my contemporaries. It is only now that I can appreciate the rare educational opportunity I experienced at Cal Poly during the time I attended.

My desire is to give back at least a small contribution to the profession of landscape architecture through this book.

— Scott Bradstreet

1883